INSIGHT ⊙ GUIDES

RIGA
POCKET GUIDE

PLAN & BOOK
YOUR TAILOR-MADE TRIP

BRAZIL **CHILE** **ECUADOI**

TAILOR-MADE TRIPS & UNIQUE EXPERIENCES CREATED E LOCAL TRAVEL EXPERTS AT INSIGHTGUIDES.COM/HOLIDA

Insight Guides has been inspiring travellers with high-quality travel cont for over 45 years. As well as our popular guidebooks, we now offer the opportunity to book tailor-made private trips completely personalised to y needs and interests. By connecting with one of our local experts, you w directly benefit from their expertise and local know-how, helping you cre memories that will last a lifetime.

HOW INSIGHTGUIDES.COM/HOLIDAYS WORKS

STEP 1

Pick your dream destination and submit an enquiry, or modify an existing itinerary if you prefer.

STEP 2

Fill in a short form, sh details of your travel p and preferences with expert.

STEP 3

Your local expert will create your personalised itinerary, which you can amend until you are completely satisfied.

STEP 4

Book securely online. your bags and enjoy y holiday! Your local ex will be available to ar questions during you

BENEFITS OF PLANNING & BOOKING AT INSIGHTGUIDES.COM/HOLIDAYS

PLANNED BY LOCAL EXPERTS
The Insight Guides local experts are hand-picked, based on their experience in the travel industry and their impeccable standards of customer service.

SAVE TIME & MONEY
When a local expert plans your trip, you save time and money when you book, even during high season. You won't be charged for using a credit card either.

TAILOR-MADE TRIPS
Book with Insight Guides, and you will be in complete control of the planning process, from the initial selections to amending your final itinerary.

BOOK & TRAVEL STRESS-FREE
Enjoy stress-free travel when you use the Insight Guides secure online booking platform. All bookings come with a money-back guarantee.

WHAT OTHER TRAVELLERS THINK ABOUT TRIPS BOOKED AT INSIGHTGUIDES.COM/HOLIDAYS

Trip to Vietnam

The organization was superb, the drivers professional, and accommodation quite comfortable. I was well taken care of! My thanks to your colleagues who helped make my trip to Vietnam such a great experience. My only regret is that I couldn't spend more time in the country.

Heather

★★★★★

DON'T MISS OUT
BOOK NOW AT
INSIGHTGUIDES.COM/HOLIDAYS

TOP 10 ATTRACTIONS

THE CENTRAL MARKET
One of the city's most exciting treasure troves, with a carnival vibe. See page 63.

SIGULDA
A short trip from Riga, this pretty riverside town makes a great day trip. See page 74.

THE FREEDOM MONUMENT
This 1930s monument is a revered symbol of the Latvian nation. See page 54.

THE SWEDISH GATE
A fascinating reminder of Riga's days as a prosperous Swedish port. See page 47.

DOME CATHEDRAL
Its great tower dominates the old town of Riga.
See page 39.

THE HOUSE OF BLACKHEADS
A guild of merchants once banqueted here.
See page 35.

THE NATIONAL OPERA HOUSE
This is the pride and joy of Riga. See page 55.

THE ETHNOGRAPHIC OPEN-AIR MUSEUM OF LATVIA
Discover Latvia's rich folk heritage here.
See page 69.

JŪRMALA
During the summer, beach culture takes centre stage on the Baltic coast.
See page 71.

ART NOUVEAU DISTRICT
The city centre is an architectural showcase.
See page 60.

A PERFECT DAY

9am

Central Market Tour
Start the day with a visit to the Central Market (see page 63). Each of its four original buildings still sells the originally intended products: fish, dairy, fruit and vegetables, and meat. Those brave enough might try some local delicacies.

12.30pm

Lunch
Have lunch at the elegant 'Melnie Mūki' (Black Monks) restaurant (see page 105), located in a section of a medieval convent. Look for chef's specials including international as well as Latvian staples and wash them down with one of the excellent Latvian beers.

11am

Old Riga
Head for the Old Town to visit the excellent Museum of the Occupation of Latvia, which recounts Latvia's painful history. Afterwards, take a walk around the Old Town with its medieval buildings. Don't miss Sts Peter and Paul Church, Three Brothers and the Dome Cathedral (see page 39).

10am

Culture Trail
Take a walk through the Moscow District (Maskavas Forštate) located behind the market, with its 19th-century wooden houses and the warehouse quarter (Spiķeri), full of trendy cafés, bars, clubs and art galleries. If you fancy a museum, there is the small but eye-opening Riga Ghetto and Latvian Holocaust Museum (see page 63).

IN **RIGA**

2pm

Art Nouveau

Head to the Art Nouveau District (see page 60) and get to know one of the most beautiful parts of the city. The flamboyant style easily recognised in the facades of the buildings along Elizabetes or Albert streets became a symbol of Riga's golden age when, at the end of the 19th century, Riga's wealth was at its zenith. Visit the Riga Art Nouveau Museum (see page 61) on Alberta street to see a fully furnished apartment of the time; then take a break in one of the district's welcoming cafés.

5pm

Shopping

Explore the pleasant parks that form a green strip near the city centre. Don't miss the Freedom Monument and Laima Clock (see page 54). For shopping, go to trendy Bergs Bazaar (see page 56) to buy hand-made chocolates, clothing and furs, beautiful soaps and local linens.

8pm

Dinner in the park

Round up the day at Bibliotēka restaurant located in the beautiful Vērmane Park. Its interior resembles the old library while the chef serves excellent contemporary Latvian cuisine rich in flavour and texture. Enjoy the lush greenery of the park trough large panoramic windows.

10.30pm

A night on the town

Start with a few post-dinner drinks in Balzambārs, a trendy bar beside the Dome Cathedral. Then move on to Coyote Fly for some dancing or if you prefer, the Royal Casino, open 24-hours. Note that if you plan to go here, you'll need to bring your passport and leave it at the door.

CONTENTS

INTRODUCTION

From its medieval golden age as the largest city in the Swedish Empire to its heyday in the early 20th century as an economic powerhouse and Russia's third-largest port, Riga has long been a symbol of commerce and cosmopolitan living. A mere decade after becoming the capital of an independent Latvia, the citizens of 1930s Riga enjoyed one of the highest standards of living in Europe. Yet, as Western nations enjoyed the fruits of freedom and democracy during the Cold War, Latvia's only major metropolis languished behind the Iron Curtain – its past glory all but forgotten – until now.

Stereotypes about Eastern Europe die hard and, although much of the world has discovered the grandeur of cities such as Prague and Budapest, the Latvian capital is still relatively unknown. That said, low-cost airlines have made once-distant Riga an increasingly attractive destination.

Located near the mouth of the River Daugava on the Baltic Sea, Riga has a beautiful medieval old town surrounded by a meandering canal, lush, manicured parks and impressive tree-lined boulevards. Its Gothic church spires and yellow crusader castle are the first architectural treasures one notices, but soon visitors are overwhelmed by its elaborate art nouveau edifices which comprise nearly a third of the city's buildings.

LAND AND PEOPLE

Riga covers an area of 300 sq km (115 sq miles) and is home to more than a third of Latvia's 1.95 million inhabitants. The city is divided by the 500m (1,640ft)-wide River Daugava, and most of the historical sights lie on the right bank around the old town, known as *Vecrīga*. Here you will find Dutch Renaissance apartment

Art Nouveau buildings are common

houses, 13th-century churches and picturesque squares that can compete with the finest Europe has to offer. Leave its medieval core and you will discover a modern, cosmopolitan city with busy boulevards, parks designed in the 19th century, and the most concentrated collection of art nouveau buildings found anywhere on the European continent. Best of all, Riga gives off a big-city feel without actually being one. Indeed, most of its historical attractions can be reached on foot or by a short tram ride.

Latvia's oldest city has taken the best from its Baltic neighbours. Between the cool Estonians and the excitable Lithuanians, Latvians take the middle ground. They are diligent to a fault and even their ancient folk songs take a scornful view of idleness. Unless actively engaged in conversation, or fortified with a drink or two, most Latvians are reserved in public and seldom talk to strangers. However, once the ice is broken, there's no holding them back.

Take a boat out on the canal

    Due to the russification policies of the USSR, Russians, who currently make up 25 percent of Latvia's population, now out-number Latvians in the capital and make up the fourth-largest ethnic group in the region. They are considered to be much more boisterous than the Balts, and are often regarded as open and willing to meet new people. But their presence is a continuing bone of contention. Tens of thousands of Latvians were deported to Siberia during and after World War II, never to be heard from again, and there was a huge, engineered influx of Russian-speakers from the USSR. The Soviets delib-erately attempted to dilute the native population to quell resistance, and thousands of new jobs were offered solely to immigrants from other republics within the Soviet Union. Use of the Latvian language was discouraged in public life and Latvians essentially became second-class citizens. This Soviet legacy is a touchy subject with Latvians, who nearly became a minority in their own nation. Although Balkan-style ethnic conflict will never become a reality in pragmatist Latvia, relations between these two groups can best be described as cordial, but icy.

PRESENT AND FUTURE

But most Latvians are willing to put the past behind them. Now citizens of the EU, competition in any business in Riga is fierce, and the number and variety of shops, restaurants and clubs around town is staggering. Then, after drinks at a trendy cocktail bar or Irish pub, you can take advantage of the city's infamous clubs that don't close their doors until their patrons decide to leave. Twenty-four-hour bars and casinos are also a permanent fixture of this city that refuses to sleep and unsurprisingly, Riga is highly popular with stag parties.

Construction cranes loom large all over the city and the sights, sounds and smells of renovation are a part of daily life here. Rampant corruption means that much of this growth has gone unchecked and for a time it appeared that Riga might even lose its hallowed status as a Unesco World Heritage Site. Although much of the damage has already been done, new legislation and higher salaries have been implemented to prevent further urban sprawl and the destruction of historic buildings and neighbourhoods, many of which have now been renovated with entire neighbourhoods being revitalised.

The Euro

After swapping Latvian lats (Ls) for euros in 2014, prices in Latvia have risen significantly. However, that said Riga remains substantially cheaper than many of its western counterparts. It is still possible to have a basic meal in the city centre for about 7–10 euros.

A BRIEF HISTORY

Riga's history is complex, but much of it can be explained by the city's chief purpose as the focal point of commerce in the region. Since its founding in 1201, the port city has been coveted by all of its neighbouring powers. Its prime location at the mouth of the River Daugava on the Baltic Sea ensured its status as a window on the vast resources of the Russian lands in the east, and its natural harbour guaranteed a constant flow of luxury goods from the west. This has been the key to its prosperity and also its curse.

On the eve of Riga's founding, four tribal kingdoms coexisted on the territory that is now Latvia. These ancient ancestors of

Riga and the River Daugava, a copperplate engraving from 1638

the Latvians led a sedentary life and spoke a Baltic language similar to that used by Lithuanian and Prussian tribes to the south. A fifth group of inhabitants called the Livs had settled in small fishing villages along the coastline and spoke a Finno-Ugric language closely related to that spoken by present-day Estonians. For centuries, these groups lived and fought among one another on these shores, often trading amber, honey and animal skins with far-flung cultures around Europe and even the Middle East. Tacitus and Herodotus both mention the amber routes of antiquity and their origin in the Baltic lands.

THE NORTHERN CRUSADE
By the 12th century, the raids of barbarous Vikings were no longer a threat, but a new foe surfaced, disguised as messengers of Christ. German traders began arriving at the mouth of the River Daugava in the 1100s and took back to their native cities stories of the prosperous lands in the north populated by pagan savages. Before long, merchants and priests arrived in droves, but it wasn't until Bishop Albert von Buxhoevden from Bremen obtained a papal bull to begin a church-sanctioned crusade against the infidels that the real trouble began.

Albert did not want to repeat the mistake of his predecessor, Bishop Berthold of Hanover, who was stabbed with a spear and literally torn to pieces by the Livs. Upon his arrival in 1201, Albert began construction of a fortress to protect himself and his men, and this year is widely accepted as the official date of the founding of Riga. Facing opposition by volatile local tribes, Albert created the Livonian Order the following year, which is also known as the Order of the Brotherhood of the Sword.

In the coming decades Riga was a frequent target of raiding parties by indigenous tribes, but because of its excellent fortifications the city was never taken. The Order continued to conquer the lands of the four Latvian tribes – the Cours, Semigallians, Selonians and Letts – often pitting one against the other. The tribes lacked unity and began to fall one by one until they were all subjugated, by 1290. The Order, however, was no match for the neighbouring Lithuanians, who inflicted devastating defeats upon them in 1236 and 1260 with the help of rebellious Latvian tribes.

The next two centuries were marked by the increasing prosperity of Riga, and the ceaseless struggle for power between the Bishop of Riga, the town council and the Order. The hated Order gained the upper hand due to its size and military strength, but its forays into the Russian lands to the east met with disaster at the hands of Alexander Nevski at Lake Peipus. In 1410 at the Battle of Tannenberg, overwhelming Polish and Lithuanian forces decisively beat the Teutonic Order, to which the Livonian

⊘ HANSEATIC LEAGUE

Riga's wealth in the late Middle Ages was in part due to its joining in 1282 of the Hanseatic League, Europe's first free-trade organisation. The league was started by German merchant societies (Hanse) to protect the herring trade in Lübeck and its vital salt suppliers in Hamburg. The alliance soon developed into a powerful confederation of more than 150 port-cities that came to control the shipping of fish, flax, fur, grain, honey and timber from Russia and the Baltics, and cloth and other goods manufactured by Flemish and English guilds. Riga had exclusive rights to transport goods along the River Daugava, and Livonia had its own Hanseatic diet or parliament. The Hansa merchants left their mark on the towns and cities where they were established and much of Old Riga is characterised by the red-brick, step-gabled buildings common to Hansa ports.

Order also belonged. More crusaders were eventually assembled and the Livonian Order once again conquered Riga in 1491.

POLES AND SWEDES

Martin Luther's Reformation arrived in Riga in 1522 and was widely embraced by the populace. The bishop of Riga lost his credibility and the town council became the most powerful force in local politics. The old Order no longer

Merchant statue on the 14th-century House of Blackheads

served much purpose, as most of its knights had become wealthy landowners. Increasing Russian raids from the east caused the last grand master of the Order to swear his allegiance to the Polish king in 1561. In return, the grand master was given land in western Livonia, which became the Duchy of Courland. The Livonian Order ceased to exist, but Riga was forced to accept Polish rule and the unpopular Catholic faith.

In 1600, war erupted between Poland and Sweden and by 1621, Gustavus Adolphus's forces had laid siege to Riga. The city eventually surrendered to the Swedish king and a new era of learning, public works and increased trade began. Schools and hospitals were built across Swedish Livonia, the first newspaper was published, the first code of laws was implemented and the Bible was translated into Latvian. Russian troops attacked the city in 1656, but despite overwhelming odds, the city's defenders thwarted the Russians' efforts, forcing them to retreat. Relative peace ruled the realm for roughly another half century. At this time, Riga was the largest city in the Swedish Empire, which included much of present-day Scandinavia, Latvia, Estonia and parts of Poland and Germany.

THE RUSSIAN EMPIRE

By 1700, the Russian Empire was expanding and it desperately wanted a foothold on the Baltic Sea, which was completely dominated by the Kingdom of Sweden. The Great Northern War between the two powers would engulf the region for more than 20 years, laying waste to the once prosperous lands of what is now Latvia. Less than 100,000 inhabitants of Livonia would survive the carnage and the ensuing plague.

In the middle of the night on 6 April 1709, an omen of terrible things to come awoke the citizens of Riga. A huge ice sheet broke free in the river causing a major flood that left much of the city under water. By October, Russian forces had reached the gates of the city. After seven months of siege and fierce canon bombardment, Riga surrendered to the armies of Peter the Great in June 1710. By the end of the century all of Livonia had been conquered by Russia. In Riga, the Germans of the town council and the guilds began excluding Latvians from all positions of power, while the land barons gained complete control of their Latvian serfs, abusing

Courland's colonies

In the 1640s, Duke Jacob of Courland (1610–82) owned colonies in Gambia, Africa, and the island of Tobago in the Caribbean. He presided over a vast maritime fleet and was considered to be one of the wealthiest Europeans of his day. Today, Tobago's Great Courland Bay is a testament to its short-lived colonisation by Latvians and Baltic Germans.

and torturing them at will and in some cases even selling and trading them as slaves.

THE 19TH CENTURY AND THE LATVIAN AWAKENING

The 19th century brought both hardship and prosperity to Riga. Believing Napoleon's troops were headed for the city, a hasty decision was made by local Russian commanders to raze the wooden buildings of the suburbs. A small contingent of Napoleon's forces did eventually reach Riga, but the majority of his army headed directly for Moscow, instead of via the Baltics to St Petersburg, as many had feared. Riga was never taken.

Despite the abolition of serfdom in Latvia, peasant revolts erupted in the countryside for two years from 1817. Former serfs were no longer obliged to work the land, but they had nowhere to go and were forbidden from owning property, which effectively worsened their lot. By the second half of the century a national awakening began as intellectuals started educating the masses about their rights. The first Latvian newspapers were published and the first Latvian Song Festival was held in 1873. Meanwhile the city experienced a boom time and it grew to become the third-largest port city in the Russian Empire. The archaic prohibition against constructing stone buildings outside the city walls was lifted and the ancient walls and ramparts were torn down. It was during this period of unprecedented wealth and expansion that much of the city took on its current appearance.

THE 20TH CENTURY

In 1901 the city celebrated its 700th anniversary with much fanfare, but only four years later revolution overwhelmed Riga. Fifty thousand demonstrators took to the streets, provoking a brutal crackdown on striking factory workers. The tsar granted concessions, but also sent 'punishment brigades' to the region which executed nearly 2,000 Latvians.

World War I brought both pain and opportunity. By 1915, half of Latvian territory was occupied by German forces and Russia allowed Latvians to raise an army to defend the country from invaders. On 18 November 1918, just seven days after Germany surrendered, a congress of Latvian intellectuals seized the opportunity and declared Latvia's independence. But the euphoria was short-lived and by 1919, Riga was captured by Russian Red forces. With renegade German troops, the Latvians repelled the communists, but then fought one another for control of the country. The Germans were eventually defeated and the Soviet Union signed a peace treaty in 1921 and withdrew its forces.

Although the country was devastated by yet another war, the economy quickly rebounded and, by the 1930s, Latvia enjoyed one of the highest standards of living in Europe. Frustrated with the incessant squabbles of parliamentarians, one of

Latvia's founding fathers, Kārlis Ulmanis, staged a blood-
less coup in 1934 and set up a dictatorship. Democracy hadn't
lasted long, but the new regime would only survive another six
years. Larger forces were at play.

In 1939 Nazi Germany and the Soviet Union signed the
Molotov–Ribbentrop pact, which divided Eastern Europe into
German and Soviet spheres of influence. Given an ultimatum by
the Soviets to allow its army to create bases in Latvia or go to war,
Ulmanis ordered Latvian troops to stand down fearing a blood-
bath. Latvia was invaded, and soon arrests, executions, torture
and deportations to Siberia befell its citizens. Germany invaded a
year later. For the next three years, Latvia was under Nazi occupation, a time during which Latvian Jewry was all but destroyed
and men and boys were conscripted into the German army. By
the end of the summer of 1944, much of Latvia had been retaken
by the Soviets, leading to a mass exodus of refugees to the West.

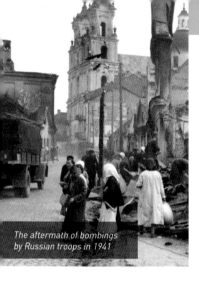
The aftermath of bombings by Russian troops in 1941

Latvia was illegally annexed by the USSR and remained a captive nation for nearly half a century.

Over the next five decades, collectivisation was enforced and tens of thousands of Latvians were herded like animals into rail boxcars and shipped to Siberia to die. Soviet citizens from around the union were encouraged to move to Latvia in a deliberate attempt to make Latvians a minority in their own nation. Russian became the dominant language of bureaucracy and any displays of patriotism were punished severely. Russian-speakers became the majority in Riga, and unchecked industrial growth polluted the nation's soil and waterways.

The new policies of *glasnost* and *perestroika* introduced by the Soviet President Mikhail Gorbachev gained popularity in the 1980s and inspired Latvians to begin protesting against the regime. Dates of mass deportations to Siberia were commemorated, and activists founded the Latvian Popular Front, which in 1989 called for full independence. That same year, some two million Estonians, Latvians and Lithuanians formed a human chain that stretched from Vilnius to Tallinn to protest the 50th anniversary of the Molotov–Ribbentrop Pact.

In 1991, seizing an opportunity to strike while the world's attention was distracted by the first Gulf War, Soviet troops moved in. In Riga, people erected barricades to protect the parliament, and a Soviet assault on the Interior Ministry resulted in the deaths of five people. In a referendum held in March, Latvians voted overwhelmingly in favour of independence. By 21 August, a coup in Moscow against President Gorbachev had collapsed and the Latvian parliament voted to immediately restore independence, which was recognised by the USSR two weeks later. Latvia was free.

AFTER INDEPENDENCE

The unity experienced during the days of the barricades soon faded and parliament became rife with partisanship, double-dealing and political scandals. Privatisation occurred rapidly, but corruption often benefited individuals and special interests, not the nation as a whole. Latvia's multi-party system led to

⊙ THE FATE OF THE JEWISH GHETTOES

Before World War II there were around 45,000 Jews in Riga, just over 10 percent of the population. By 1945 about 150 remained. Several thousand Jews were immediately shot by the Einsatzgruppen (mobile killing units), aided by Latvian auxiliaries, after German troops entered the city in July 1941. The rest were driven into a ghetto behind the station around Lāčplēša and Ludzas streets, which was sealed in October that year. Some 20,000 Jews from Germany, Austria, Bohemia and Moravia were also brought to Riga and sealed in a separate ghetto. Later that year, on just two days, around 25,000 ghetto Jews were murdered in the Rumbula forest 8km (5 miles) southeast of the city. After the war many Jews returned to Latvia and by the time of independence in 1989 there were around 23,000 registered in Riga, though the number has since fallen due to emigration.

Girls in traditional dress

the creation of unstable coalitions and the parliament presided over the collapse of 11 governments in 13 years. Fortunately, most parties could agree on two important goals – Nato and the European Union. Latvia became a member of both in 2004.

The 2008 world financial crisis hit Latvia hard, causing massive unemployment (over 20 percent), a €7.5bn loan from the IMF, followed by drastic austerity measures and the subsequent collapse of the government. Although the economy rebounded in 2012 and in 2014 Latvia adopted the euro, some problems remain, namely high unemployment, a shrinking population (Latvia has lost over 600,000 citizens since 1989), political instability and tensions with Russia over the conflict in Ukraine, as Latvians fear their hard-won independence may once more be under threat. In 2015, Latvia asked for a permanent presence of NATO troops on its soil and in 2017, NATO deployed a multinational battle group in the country.

HISTORICAL LANDMARKS

2500 BC The ancestors of modern Latvians arrive on the Baltic Sea.

1100s German traders appear by the River Daugava.

1201 Bishop Albert founds the city of Riga.

1202 The Livonian Order is created with the pope's blessing in Riga.

1282 Riga joins the Hanseatic League.

1522 The Reformation arrives in Riga, bringing with it social unrest.

1561 The Livonian Order ceases to exist.

1621 Sweden emerges victorious from the Polish-Swedish war. Golden age begins.

1710 Riga surrenders to Peter the Great of Russia.

1819 Serfdom is abolished.

1905 The first Russian Revolution fails and hundreds of people are brutally executed.

1918 Independence proclaimed by congress of Latvian intelligentsia.

1919 Russian Red forces take Riga and fledgling government flees.

1921 Latvian independence is recognised by the USSR.

1940 The Soviet Union invades Latvia.

1941 The Nazis drive out the Soviets.

1944 The Red Army once again occupies most of Latvia, and at the end of the war Latvia is left on the wrong side of the Iron Curtain.

1989 Latvian Popular Front calls for full independence.

1991 Latvia declares its independence.

1994 The last Soviet troops withdraw.

2004 Latvia joins Nato and the EU.

2008 A €7.5bn rescue package is approved by the IMF and the EU. Austerity measures provoke social unrest and result in the fall of the government.

2014 The euro is adopted, pushing prices up.

2017 NATO troops deploy in Latvia as part of NATO Enhanced Forward Presence.

2019 In January, Arturs Krišjānis Kariņš (New Unity) becomes prime minister following the October 2018 parliamentary election.

Aerial view of Riga's Old Town and Dome Cathedral

WHERE TO GO

By Baltic standards Riga is a huge city, but in truth many of its most interesting sights are easily accessible on foot or by a short tram ride. A stroll through the meandering cobblestone streets of Old Riga, a ride to the top of St Peter's spire for fantastic views of terracotta roofs, and a tour of the city centre's incredible art nouveau buildings are all highlights of a trip to the Latvian capital. For the sake of expediency, this guide divides the old town into two sections, which are followed by descriptions of the surrounding ring of boulevards and parks. The most noteworthy regions of the city centre or 'new city' have also been listed, as are suburban places of interest. Intrepid travellers can also take excursions to crusader castle ruins and restored palaces in the countryside.

OLD RIGA: SOUTHERN HALF

In the 800 years since its founding, Riga has experienced dramatic changes at the hands of both foreign armies and local town planners but, for the most part, its winding streets haven't changed their course or, for that matter, their names. Most of the old town's bustling streets and alleyways still bear the names that indicated the trades of their early inhabitants, such as Painters', Merchants' and Blacksmiths' streets. We'll start south of Lime Street (Kaļķu iela), the dividing line of Old Riga, where the city began its existence as a small fishing village populated by Liv tribesmen, around what is now **Albert Square** (Alberta laukums).

It certainly isn't one of the prettiest squares the city has to offer but it does provide a unique glimpse of Riga's past, present and future. From here you can view restored 17th-century warehouses, Cold War-era Soviet architecture, the crumbling husks of derelict apartment buildings and, in the distance, the glass-and-steel façade of a cinema complex.

ALKSNĀJA, PEITAVAS AND MĀRSTAĻU STREETS

Walk past graffitied warehouses from the 16th to 18th centuries on Alksnāja iela until you reach the **Latvian Sports Museum** (www.sportamuzejs.lv; Tue–Fri 10am–5pm, Sat 11am–6pm; guided tours upon previous booking), which celebrates the nation's best athletes. Along the way, note the bas-reliefs of plants and animals above the huge wooden warehouse doors, which informed the mostly illiterate populace of the items stored within: clusters of grapes denoted wines and a camel symbolised exotic spices from the east. Similar signs can be seen throughout Old Riga. Ahead on the left is the **Reformation Church** (Reformātu baznīca), which was built from 1727 to 1733. One of the few baroque-style houses of worship in the city, for a time it also had the distinction of having the only Calvinist congregation in Latvia. The Soviets used it as a recording studio and student disco, but after independence the ground floor was turned into a concert hall and the cellar a string of nightclubs.

Colourful Mārstaļu Street

Across the street is the **Latvian Photography Museum** (Latvijas fotogrāfijas muzejs; www.fotomuzejs.lv; Wed, Fri–Sun 10am–5pm, Thu noon–7pm), which has a collection of late 19th-century photographs of the rural landscape, as well as some striking images from World War I. The highlight of the museum is the Minox spy camera, produced in Latvia just prior to the war and later manufactured by the famous German firm, Leica.

Inside the synagogue

One block over on Peitavas iela is Riga's only surviving **synagogue** (Sinagoga; www.jews.lv; Mon–Fri from 7.30am until after the evening prayers, Sun from 8.30am; free), built in 1904. It was spared the fate of other Jewish houses of worship due to its close proximity to houses in Old Riga. Fearing an uncontrollable blaze if they torched it, the Nazis used it instead as a warehouse.

Further up Mārstaļu, just before the river, you'll see one of the last remaining fragments of the old town's original **city walls** to the left and the **Dannenstern House** on the right. Built in 1696 by a wealthy Dutch merchant, it was the largest residence at the time in Riga. Its owner oversaw a fleet of 150 ships and was later given a noble title by the king of Sweden. Due to a lack of space in the medieval city, most homes also served as warehouses, which is clear to anyone who looks at this massive, multi-storeyed structure. Ahead is the river promenade, which leads to the **1905 Revolution monument** to the left. Nearly 2,000 people across Latvia were killed in the aftermath of the failed uprising.

On the opposite end of Mārstaļu is one of the best examples of both Dutch Classical and baroque architecture in Riga – the **Reutern House** (Reiterna nams), completed in 1685. Of particular interest is the depiction of a lion pouncing on a bear at the top, which was the owner's cheeky way of celebrating the victory of Sweden over Russia. The ground floor now houses a rock bar.

ST JOHN'S AND BEYOND

Just past the aptly named Sinners' Street (Grēcinieku iela), home to some of the city's hottest nightclubs and bars, you'll see the bright terracotta tiles and green neo-Gothic spire of **St John's Church** (Jāņa baznīca; Mon–Sat 10am–6pm, Sun 2–6pm; free), built in the 13th century. Like most Lutheran churches, its interior is for the most part austere, but its elaborate vaulted ceiling is considered to be one of the most beautiful in the Baltic region. Two medieval monks chose to be immured in the southern wall in the hope of becoming saints and were fed by passers-by through two window grates that are still visible from the street. They didn't survive very long and were never canonised

Wagner at work

Nearly bankrupt and desperate for work, Richard Wagner travelled to Riga in 1837, where he worked as the musical director of the German Theatre, conducted many of Beethoven's symphonies and began writing *Rienzi, the Last of the Tribunes*. After only two seasons, he made a hasty escape from his creditors in 1839, leaving the city for London and Paris under cover of darkness. The stormy waters of the Baltic Sea later served as his inspiration for the *Flying Dutchman*.

because they did it for their own glory and not for the glory of God. Their bodies were rediscovered in the 19th century after the spire collapsed causing minor damage to the building. Repairs were made and they were left behind the wall. Just behind the building is the picturesque **John's Courtyard** (Jāņa sēta), home to bars, clubs and beer gardens. Here you can see another fragment of Riga's old town walls, draped with colourful flowers in summer.

Bremen Town Musicians political monument

Beyond the courtyard at No. 13 on Wagner Street (Vāgnera iela) is the **Museum of Pharmacy** (Farmācijas muzejs; www. mvm.lv; Tue–Sat 10am–6pm, Sun until 4pm), which displays old bottles, many of which still contain their original ingredients. Of equal significance is the building's rococo doorway, one of the few examples of this style in Riga. Further up the street at No. 4 is the **Wagner Concert Hall** (Vāgnera zāle) where the troubled composer conducted for two years (see page 30).

Opposite the church is a statue of the **Bremen Town Musicians** from the Grimm fairytale. It was a gift from the city of Bremen, another Hanseatic city and home of Bishop Albert (1165–1229), founder of Riga. Just behind the church on the corner of Jāņa and Kalēju streets is arguably Old Riga's most beautiful art nouveau building. Built in 1903, it's a great example of Biological Romanticism.

The yellow building next to the church is **Ecke's Convent** (Ekes konventa ēka), which once belonged to a Riga mayor of the same name. Embroiled in an embezzlement scandal in 1596, he decided to curry favour with the townspeople by donating the building to impoverished widows. A hotel and restaurant now occupy its floors, but its most interesting asset is a bas-relief of Jesus and the Sinner on its façade.

The next building down the street is also a gate to the **Convent Yard** (Konventa sēta), which is an ensemble of several medieval buildings confined by other structures in a quaint courtyard once used to house the poor and disabled of Riga. It is now a hotel, which rents out space to souvenir shops, cafés and the **Riga Porcelain Museum** Ⓐ (Rīgas pocelāna muzejs; http://porcelanamuzejs.riga.lv; Tue–Sun 11am–6pm, May–Sept Wed until 7pm), whose main claim to fame is an exhibit of 19th-century ceramics; it also has a huge vase bearing the likeness of Stalin. For a small charge, children can try their hands at pottery on the premises.

A few houses down the street, past the numerous amber stalls, is the **Museum of Decorative Arts and Design** (Dekoratīvās mākslas un dizaina muzejs; www.lnmm.lv; Tue, Thu–Sun 11am–5pm, Wed until 7pm). Of more interest than the actual exhibits is the first building, which was once the chapel of the Livonian Order's castle and the city's first church, St George's (Jura baznīca). The castle was destroyed by the townspeople, but the chapel was unharmed and, to this day, is considered by many Latvians to be a source of supernatural energy.

On the other side of the street is Riga's tallest medieval structure, **St Peter's Church** Ⓑ (Pēterbaznīca; http://peter baznica.riga.lv; Sept–Apr Tue–Sat 10am–6pm, Sun noon–6pm, May–Aug until 7pm). Although the exact date of its construction is unknown, St Peter's was mentioned in chronicles in 1209. It was later enlarged and by 1491 its soaring steeple was completed.

Unfortunately, the steeple was beset by a series of disasters. It collapsed in 1666 killing townspeople below, and a decade into its reconstruction it burned down. When it was finally rebuilt in 1690 it was the tallest wooden church steeple in Europe, but it was once again engulfed in flames in 1721. Peter the Great, who was visiting Riga at the time, ordered the steeple to be rebuilt, and by 1746 it reached an impressive height of 127m (415ft). The architect drank a glass of wine at the top and dropped it to the ground, believing that the number of shards it broke into would be the number of centuries it would survive. Sadly, a pile of hay softened the blow and it only broke in two. Nearly two centuries later in 1941, it was hit by a bomb and collapsed in flames. The current steeple was completed in 1973 and the ritual was repeated – to the delight of all, the glass smashed into thousands of pieces. For €9 you can take the lift up to the observation deck for excellent views and visit the church and the crypt.

Further up the road is a lovely building topped with Dionysus holding a cluster of grapes. It was here that the Jewish-American photographer Philippe Halsman (1906–79), friend of Albert Einstein and Salvador Dalí, lived until 1929. It also has

St Peter's Church steeple

the distinction of being the first of many art nouveau buildings built in Riga. Today it is home to an American restaurant chain.

TOWN HALL SQUARE

To the left you'll see the baroque-style tower of the reconstructed **Town Hall** (Rātsnams), completed in 2004. The original building, dating from 1334, was demolished in 1750 to make room for a larger structure. Like most of the ancient square, which served as both marketplace and punishment venue, it was levelled during World War II. This recreation of the original building – with additional third floor and modern wing – is once again the seat of city government. A subterranean passageway is home to shops and a 3,500-year-old section of an oak tree found under the building's foundations.

House of the Blackheads at night

In the centre of the square is a statue of **St Roland** (Rolands) clad in a suit of armour, holding a sword in one hand and a shield bearing Riga's coat of arms in the other. Dying a martyr's death at the Battle of Roncesvals in 778, he was Charlemagne's favourite nephew and came to symbolise justice in many cities inhabited by Germans, of which Riga was no exception. The original statue was slightly damaged during the war and is on display in St Peter's, safe from the elements.

Behind Roland is the **House of Blackheads ☉** (Melngalvju nams), another building to rise from the ashes of Soviet bombings. The ancient 14th-century building once housed a guild of unmarried merchants whose bacchanalian feasts became the stuff of legend. It is rumoured that monarchs and nobil-

ity, including Catherine the Great, secretly participated in these events. Most scholars believe that the building derives its name from either the black caps worn by its members or from its patron saint Mauritius, a Moor.

Behind the building on the corner is the **Mentzendorff House** (Mencendorfa nams; www.mencendorfanams.com; Wed–Sun 11am–5pm), dating from 1695. It illustrates the lifestyle of 17th- and 18th-century Riga merchants. During restoration, builders discovered wonderful frescoes on the walls and ceilings under layers of Soviet paint. The interior

Latvian riflemen monument

was completed with historical artefacts from the Museum of the History of Riga and Navigation.

Back on the square is the unmistakable Soviet black box constructed in 1970 as a museum dedicated to the Latvian Red Riflemen who fought during the Russian Civil War. Today, its unattractive architecture provides an appropriate venue for the **Museum of the Occupation of Latvia**  (Latvijas okupācijas muzejs; http://okupacijasmuzejs.lv; daily 11am–6pm; donation). Inside you'll find documents and photographs that chronicle Latvia's occupation by the Soviet Union and Nazi Germany. A gulag barracks has also been reconstructed to illustrate the terrible living conditions many Latvians faced after being deported to Siberia in cattle cars.

On the other side of the museum is a red granite monument now dedicated to all the **Latvian riflemen** who fought during World War I. Desperate for more troops, the tsar allowed the creation of a Latvian army to fight against the Germans, but when the revolution broke out some joined the Reds. An elite few of the Latvian Red Riflemen became the private bodyguard of Lenin. Soldiers from both sides joined Latvia's cause after independence was declared in 1918. Beside the monument you can begin organised walking and bus tours of the city.

OLD RIGA: NORTHERN HALF

Just before the Town Hall Square is Trash Street (Krāmu iela), which, contrary to its misguided name, affords passers-by one of the most spectacular views of Dome Cathedral. Heading towards the church on the right side is Riga's narrowest street, **Rozena iela**, which is made more picturesque by a medieval-style restaurant. On the right is the **Museum of Barricades of 1991** (1991. gada barikāžu muzejs; http://barikades.lv; Mon–Fri 10am–5pm; free), which tells the story of how Latvians from across the country flocked to the city to protect it against elite Soviet OMON forces in January and August 1991. Giant concrete slabs were erected around Old Riga and lorry drivers and even farmers on tractors deposited their vehicles at strategic locations to deny tanks entry.

Around the corner on Jauniela is another excellent example of art nouveau, built in 1903 and famous for its huge face above the entrance. Across the street in a courtyard once used as a beer garden you can see **tombstones** that once paved the floor of the cathedral. In the left corner is a small bas-relief of the crucifixion painted silver, which is also believed to have once been located indoors. Below you can see the ground level of Riga before floods, fires

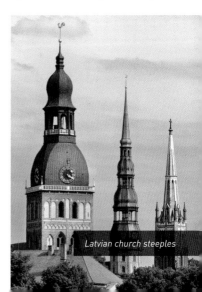

Latvian church steeples

Russian occupation

When Russian troops captured Riga in 1710, it was a huge feather in Peter the Great's cap. The tsar is said to have visited the city often and was given a gift of a palace by the local magistrate, which is still visible, albeit in modified form, at No. 9 Palasta in Old Riga.

and 800 years of habitation took their toll.

Ahead is a former palace built in the late 1600s (and reconstructed several times), which has played host to 18th- and 19th-century royalty, including Peter the Great and Catherine the Great. Beyond the palace is a tiny shed which is probably the only medieval carriage house in Riga still in existence.

Just before **Herder Square** (Herdera laukums), named after the influential German philosopher Johann Gotfried Herder (1744–1803) who once taught at the Dome School, is one of the country's best and oldest museums, the **Museum of the History of Riga and Navigation** (Rīgas vēstures un kuģniecības muzejs; www.riga muz.lv; May–Sept daily 10am–5pm, Oct–Apr Wed–Sun 11am–5pm). Founded under a different name in 1773, it moved into the current building in 1891. Inside is an eclectic collection of all things Rigan, including Bronze Age artefacts, suits of armour, religious items, medieval documents, memorabilia from the 1920s and 1930s, and plenty of other curiosities.

DOME SQUARE (DOMA LAUKUMS)

Seven streets converge at this beautiful square that is now the heart and soul of Old Riga. Yet oddly, it didn't even exist only a century ago. Ancient houses once covered the square, some of which were demolished by the city to grant greater access to the cathedral, and the rest fell victim to bombing raids during World

War II. Today, if you look closely at the patterns of the cobble-stones you can discern the outlines of the buildings that once stood in the shadow of the largest house of worship in the Baltics. In the centre of the square is a bronze disc commemorating the city's inclusion on Unesco's list of World Heritage Sites. It is also at this point that you can see three church spires.

Construction of **Dome Cathedral** Ⓔ (Rīgas Doms or Doma baznīca; www.doms.lv; May–Sept Mon–Tue and Sat 9am–6pm, Wed and Fri 9am–5pm, Thu 9am–5.30pm, Sun 2–5pm, Oct–Apr Mon–Sat 10am–5pm, Sun 2–5pm) began at the behest of Riga's founder, Bishop Albert (see page 40), in 1211, but like all of the city's churches it was enlarged and embellished over the years. Even the golden numerals on the east side of the building, indicating the year 1721, only give evidence of the

Relaxing in Dome Square

completion of repairs to the church, which suffered during Peter the Great's siege of the city in 1709. It was also damaged by a devastating flood that same year and a small plaque on the far right side of the church before the altar marks the level that the water reached. Its many treasures were looted during the Reformation riots of the 1520s and its elaborately

⊙ BISHOP ALBERT AND THE NORTHERN CRUSADE

Albert von Buxhoevden (1165–1229) is credited with the founding of Riga in 1201 when he ordered the construction of a fortification to protect himself and his crusaders from local pagan tribes. Born into a prominent family – the Buxhoevdens of northern Germany – he was a member of the clergy in Bremen before being named bishop of Livonia.

Eager to avoid the fate of his predecessor, who was torn to pieces in a battle with a Liv tribe, he garnered the support of Pope Innocent III and King Philip of Swabia. He also obtained a papal bull to save the souls of the heathens living in the northern Baltic. With 23 ships and an army of 1,500 men, he arrived in what would become Riga.

Previous attempts to subdue the local Latvian tribes had failed. In 1202, Bishop Albert founded the Livonian Order, a permanent military monastic order that was based on the Templars. The order did battle across Latvia and parts of Estonia, building castles as they went.

By his death in 1229 Albert had founded a city and an order of knights, built fortresses and the Dome Cathedral, and attained the titles of Holy Roman Prince and Bishop of Livonia. A statue of the illustrious clergyman adorns one of the walls of the Dome Cloister.

The cathedral's original weathervane

carved pews (apart from the Blackheads' pew depicting Moors wearing turbans) 'disappeared' during its reconstruction as a concert hall during the Soviet era. Thankfully, many of the original stained-glass windows donated by the guilds and wealthy patrons have survived.

One of the cathedral's most valuable assets is its enormous **organ** embellished with ornate wood carvings. The original instrument was installed in the late 16th century and served its parishioners well for nearly 300 years until the congregation decided to commission a better one. Even the tsar donated money to the cause and by 1884 the continent's best-known firm, Walcker's of Ludwigsburg, completed the task of building the world's largest organ. The dedication was such a momentous event that Franz Liszt composed music for the occasion. The wood carvings from the 1590s were not replaced and can still be viewed today. Organ concerts are held here frequently.

Behind the cathedral is a courtyard and the **Dome Cloister** (Doma krusteja; www.rigamuz.lv; May–Sept daily 10am–5pm, Oct–Apr Wed–Sun 11am–5pm), supposedly the largest of its kind in northern Europe. Apart from excellent examples of Romanesque architecture, you can also view various out-doors exhibits, including old canon, the original copper rooster weathervane of Dome Cathedral, tombstones dating back to the 13th century and even a stained-glass depiction of Lenin.

Dome Cathedral isn't the only architectural gem on the square. Perhaps the most striking building is the Venetian Renaissance-style **Stock Exchange** (Rīgas birža) building, completed in 1855 and painted in various shades of brown and green, now housing the excellent Art Museum Riga Bourse (Mākslas muzejs Rīgas Birža; http://lnmm.lv; Tue–Thu, Sat–Sun 10am–6pm, Fri until 8pm; guided tours must be booked in advance). Opened in 2011, it harmoniously explores the links between East and West and the classics and modernity. The exhibits include a superb collection of 17th century North European school paintings as well as 18th century Meissen porcelain. There is also a museum shop and café.

Opposite the museum is the **Radio House** (Radio māja), built in 1913, with the coat of arms of Riga above the balcony where heads

Art Museum Riga Bourse

of state, including former and current presidents of Latvia, have given speeches to the masses below. It now houses offices and studios for Latvian Radio. At the east end of the square are some more examples of fantastic art nouveau architecture, as well as a wide variety of shops and cafés.

Merchants' club

The English, Irish and Scots were among the wealthiest merchants in late 19th-century Riga. The building which now houses the Danish Embassy at No. 11 Pils was built as a club for them and still displays symbols of the British Isles above the balcony: a rose, shamrock and thistle.

AROUND DOME SQUARE

Every street around the square reveals yet another medieval or art nouveau treasure. Head for the sky-blue church at the end of Pils and you'll be rewarded with vibrant cafés and more beautiful buildings. On the left is the odd-looking Danish embassy and the tiny Anglican church, **St Saviour's** (Anglikāņu baznīca). In 1857, wealthy British businessmen imported soil and bricks from England to build this small church, which still delivers services to its expatriate congregation in English.

Proceed to **Castle Square** (Pils laukums) where you'll see the bright blue **Church of Our Lady of Sorrow** (Sāpju Dievmātes katoļu baznīca; daily 7.30am–6pm). In the 18th century, the only Catholic church in Old Riga was a tiny wooden chapel that occupied this space. Austria's Kaiser Joseph II was horrified to see such a poor representation of his faith and donated a large sum of money to build the church you see now. Sadly, the Kaiser died in ignominy and subsequent royalty who donated to the church all died violent deaths, including Tsar Alexander II who was blown up by anarchists. The church was completed in 1785.

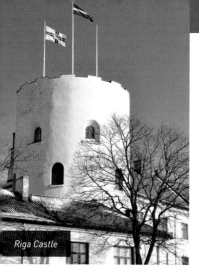
Riga Castle

If you take the small street, Poļu gāte, behind the church to the river you'll see the **Big Christopher** statue. Legend has it that after carrying a small boy across the river, who was in fact the Christ child, St Christopher returned to his cave on the embankment and discovered a pile of gold, which he used to build the city. A wooden statue first appeared by the river in the early 16th century and served as Riga's protector against the extremes of nature, especially floods. Riga's citizens would also leave offerings to him to ensure a safe journey. The current statue, encased in glass, is a replica of the original now located in the Museum of the History of Riga and Navigation.

The centrepiece of the square is, of course, the ancient Crusader Castle of the Livonian Order or **Riga Castle** (Rīgas pils). After the townspeople destroyed their first castle in 1297, the Order gained the upper hand and forced the citizens of Riga to build them a new castle at this location in 1330. It was destroyed again in 1484, but the relentless Order returned to power and yet again forced the humiliated townspeople to rebuild it in 1491. Over the years it was expanded and served as the seat of the governors of each invading power, until independence after World War I when Latvian presidents used the building as their offices – a tradition that continues today. Its recent renovation has restored it to its former glory.

If you take Jēkaba iela from Dome Square, make a left on Mazā pils to see an ensemble of three narrow medieval buildings, each erected in a different century, collectively known as the **Three Brothers ❻** (Trīs brāļi). No. 17 is the oldest residential building in the city, dating back to the 15th century. The bench outside gives an indication of the house's age; successive generations of homeowners could not afford to set aside space indoors in which to relax. No. 17's windows are tiny to avoid the 'light tax' of the time that forced residents to pay more for windows that shed light on the street. No. 19 was built in 1646 and now houses the **Latvian Architecture Museum** (Latvijas arhitektūras muzejs; www.archmuseum.lv; Mon 9am–6pm, Tue–Thu 9am–5pm, Fri until 4pm; free). The exhibits won't prove interesting unless you're into architecture, but it's worth a visit to see the ancient interior on the ground floor. The building at No. 21 is the most recent addition to the trio.

To the right on Klostera is the building that formerly housed the **Riga Lyceum**, founded by King Charles XI of Sweden in 1675. Above the doorway you'll notice the original crown of the king and a second crown of Peter the Great above it. The tsar couldn't resist the temptation to flaunt his victory over his Scandinavian foe.

Beyond the lyceum is **St Jacob's Cathedral** (Jēkaba baznīca; daily 7am–6.30pm; free), first mentioned in historical documents in 1225, the date engraved above its entrance portal. Its steeple is unusual in shape and is also the only large steeple to have a bell hanging not from within, but on the outside. Like most of the city's treasures made of precious metals, the bell was carted off to Russia and melted down during World War I, but was replaced by a new one in 2001. Outside the church on Jēkaba stands one of the concrete slabs used to protect the parliament from Soviet tanks in 1991.

To the left is a quaint street that is seldom visited by tourists, but worth a stroll, and directly ahead is the **Latvian Parliament** (Latvijas Republikas Saeima). Built in 1867 as a meeting hall for the German landed gentry who could trace their lineages back to crusading knights, it is now used by the descendants of the very people it tried to oppress. The building is closed to the public, but is impressive to look at from the outside. Particularly imposing are the iron chains surrounding the building which hang from the mouths of miniature lions' heads. Indeed, all of its features are massive, including the giant doorknockers and lampposts.

Behind the parliament is the **Arsenāls Exhibition Hall** of the Latvian National Museum of Art (Izstāžu zāle Arsenāls; www.lnmm.lv; Tue–Wed and Fri 11am–6pm, Thu until 8pm, Sat–Sun noon–5pm), housed in an impressive 19th-century customs warehouse, Riga's finest example of Russian Classicism. Most of the exhibits, including paintings by Latvian expatriates, are from the second half of the 20th century to the present.

If you head down Smilšu, one of the city's oldest streets, you'll see some excellent examples of early 20th-century architecture, most notably at Nos 2 and 8. The former was built in 1902 and exemplifies the trend of Biological Romanticism in art nouveau. With a huge peacock, trees and human forms that have roots in place of legs, the building seems almost alive. No. 8, erected in the same year, is covered with faces, gargoyles and cherubs, and has two naked women on either side of the main balcony. Make sure to take a peek at the elaborate floral designs inside the foyer.

At the end of the street is the **Powder Tower** (Pulvertornis), which may have stored gunpowder during medieval times. Dating back as far as the 14th century, it was almost completely destroyed by invading Swedish troops in 1621. It was rebuilt 30 years later with 2.5m (8ft) thick walls to avoid a repeat of this calamity. Its new construction proved successful and cheeky local masons showed off their achievement by embedding cannonballs that failed to penetrate the structure in its exterior. By the end of the 19th century, the tower had been long abandoned until a German student fraternity convinced the town council to rent them

Powder Tower

the building for a token one rouble per year. The students made a killing by selling the pigeon droppings that had piled up over decades of disuse as fertiliser. Today, the tower is a part of the **Latvian Museum of War** (Latvijas kara muzejs; daily 10am–6pm, Nov–Mar until 5pm; free), which chronicles the evolution of the Latvian army during the 20th century.

To the left on Aldaru, beyond the gravity-defying warehouse that leans over the street, is the **Swedish Gate** Ⓖ (Zviedru vārti), the only one of the many original gates in the city walls still in existence. Note the cannon embedded in the corners of the gate. Passing in front of the gate is Noise Street (Trokšņu iela), one of the city's narrowest and most picturesque streets.

To the right is the largest fragment of the once massive **old city fortress walls**. The **Ramer Guard Tower** was reconstructed during the Soviet era, so the smooth bricks betray the tower's youth, but the sight is still impressive. **Jacob's Barracks** (Jēkaba

The Swedish Gate

kazarmas), on the other side of the street, were built to house soldiers in the 18th century and continued to serve that function until Latvia regained its independence in 1991. Today they represent one of the most expensive pieces of real estate in the old town and are occupied by some of the city's trendiest shops and cafés, not to mention diplomats who live in its exclusive apartments.

LIVS' SQUARE

Although it is now one of the city's most beautiful open spaces, teeming with people, shops, cafés, beer gardens and buskers, **Livs' Square** (Līvu laukums) didn't exist prior to World War II, when the ancient buildings of the area were bombed beyond recognition. This is the best place for people watching in summer and also a great destination for soaking up the atmosphere of Old Riga.

On the western side of the square are the guildhalls, the seats of ultimate power in the city until Russian economic policies made them completely impotent in 1877. They did, however, continue to exist as a kind of German social club until Hitler ordered all of his Volk to return to the fatherland in the late 1930s.

The **Small Guild** (Mazā Ģilde) was built during the 14th century as a centre for the city's highly skilled artisans, but the present neo-Gothic structure, with its fairytale tower, was not erected until 1866. Its interior is decorated with unique tapestries and stained glass, as well as the coats of arms of several Hanseatic cities. It served various functions during Soviet times, but is now once again home to the city's Craftsmen's Guild and is also used for conferences, concerts and other special events.

The **Great Guild** (Lielā Ģilde) was home to Riga's wealthy powerbrokers, who laid down the law for all economic activities in the city. Only merchants who didn't work for wages could be admitted and the ban on the acceptance of non-German members was lifted only in the second half of the 19th century when the old 14th-century hall was replaced by the current fortress-like neo-Gothic structure. Thankfully, the ancient Münster hall, which was the venue of countless medieval events, was untouched during the upgrade. It is now used as a concert hall and is home to the Latvian Philharmonic Orchestra.

The so-called **Cat House** Ⓗ (Kaķu nams), whose image appears on countless postcards and t-shirts, is located across the street. Its striking yellow façade is reason enough to stop and look, but it's the slender black felines perched at the top of the building's towers that are the source of its fame and infamy. The story goes that the wealthy merchant who owned the building was involved in a squabble with the Great Guild and, although he fulfilled all the necessary requirements, was denied membership in the prestigious organisation. In protest, he had the cats on the towers moved so that

Executioner's ritual

Riga's medieval executioner once lived in the tiny apartment above the Swedish Gate. On the morning of a beheading, he would place a red rose on the windowsill. His sword and the mummified hand of one of his victims are on display at the Museum of the History of Riga and Navigation.

their backsides faced the guild. The guildsmen, who were the most influential citizens of the city, were outraged at the insult, but were, perhaps for the first time in their lives, completely powerless and could do nothing to convince their adversary to tame his unruly pets. Today the cats face the philharmonic hall.

CITY CENTRE

Riga's massive fortress walls and earthen ramparts faithfully served their purpose of protecting the city for half a millennium, but by the 19th century they had outlived their usefulness. Modern warfare had made them obsolete and Riga was quickly becoming one of the largest and wealthiest cities in the Russian Empire. Riga's most affluent citizens were tired of living in

The Small Guild

cramped conditions in the old town, where the filth and grime of urban living was taking its toll on the population. A change was needed. The no-man's-land that lay directly beyond the walls would be turned into artfully landscaped parks, the archaic fortifications would be torn down, the ramparts destroyed and the ban on the construction of stone buildings outside Old Riga would be lifted. The stage was set for the larg-

Cat House

est and most far-reaching construction boom in the city's history and the result is the magnificent semicircle of parks and boule-vards that surrounds the medieval core of Riga, and the priceless art nouveau masterpieces of the city centre.

KRONVALDA PARK

Named after Atis Kronvalds (1837–75), the Latvian linguist and teacher who later came to symbolise the National Awakening in the second half of the 19th century, this extensive park is divided in two by the city canal and is a favourite spot for read-ing a book on its many benches, feeding ducks at the water's edge, in-line skating on its smoothly paved walkways or simply basking in the sun. For some 70 years this prime piece of real estate between Elizabetes, Valdemāra, Kronvalda and Kalpaka boulevards was the exclusive domain of a German shooting club which created an entertainment complex that charged admission at the main entrance. The city of Riga finally bought the park in 1931 for the benefit of all of its citizens and visitors.

On the northern side of the canal is Riga's **World Trade Centre**, formerly the home of the Central Committee of the Communist Party of Latvia, which currently houses a number of embassies and international firms. Not far from the building you'll notice a concrete slab on display. It is a fragment of the **Berlin Wall**, which was donated to the city by the museum at Checkpoint Charlie. The park also displays several other different monuments, including a small pagoda (a gift from the Chinese Embassy), and the only remaining pavilion from Riga's 700th anniversary celebrations in 1901.

At the southernmost tip of the park on Valdemāra is the **National Theatre** (Nacionālais teātris) where Latvian independence was declared in November 1918 (see page 20). The building, which was designed by Augusts Reinbergs and dates back to 1902, now has a modern addition in the rear, as well as a restored art nouveau, classicist and eclectic interior.

On the other side of Kronvalda is the area of Riga where the medieval **Citadel** (Citadele) once stood. The massive fortifications thwarted the invasions of one Russian tsar and two Polish kings,

Kronvalda Park

but by the early 18th century its days were numbered. During the siege of 1709, which lasted several months, the Swedish garrison confidently held its ground until the warehouse storing all of its gunpowder was hit by artillery. The blast completely destroyed the fortress and at least 1,000 people perished in an instant. Under the Russians, the Citadel was rebuilt, but only a few of the original buildings exist today.

National Theatre

Sts Peter and Paul Church (Pētera un Pāvila baznīca) was built in 1785 as an Orthodox house of worship for Russian soldiers, but was later turned into a concert hall, which is currently named Ave Sol. In the courtyard stands the bust of Anna Kern. The wife of a local general who lived nearby, she was the inspiration for much of Alexander Pushkin's love poetry.

Sandwiched between the foreign representations on Kalpaka, or 'embassy row', on the opposite side of the park is the **Paul Stradin Museum for History of Medicine** (Paula Stradiņa medicīnas vēstures muzejs; www.mvm.lv; Tue–Wed and Fri–Sat 11am–5pm, Thu until 7pm, Sun until 4pm). The museum bears the name of Latvia's most illustrious physician and professor, Paul Stradiņš (1896–1958), and traces the history of medical practice from medieval to modern times. Among the intriguing exhibits is medical equipment that looks as if it did more harm than good and old signs warning of smallpox epidemics.

FREEDOM MONUMENT AND RIGA CANAL

A large statue of Peter the Great astride a horse once occupied the space where Latvia's most sacred monument now stands. When the tsar's statue went missing during World War I, the Latvians were in no rush to get it back. After donations were collected from all corners of the country, the **Freedom Monument** ❶ (Brīvības piemineklis), referred to endearingly by locals as Milda, was unveiled in 1935 with much fanfare. Since then it has gained the status of a national shrine, and flowers are placed at its foot each day, an act that was punishable by deportation to Siberia in Soviet times.

The first thing one notices about the monument is the tall white obelisk topped by the statue of a woman, Mother Latvia, holding three golden stars, which represent the historic regions of the country – Vidzeme, Kurzeme and Latgale. The front of the monument bears the simple inscription, 'For fatherland and freedom'. The rest of it is richly ornamented with sculptures and reliefs depicting both historic events and characters from Latvian mythology. The epic hero Lāčplēsis (the Bear Slayer) doing battle, the Song Festival march, the 1905 Revolution and the freedom fighters of 1919 are just a few of the many scenes that can be discerned on the sides of the monument.

Before you reach the monument on Aspazijas you'll see dozens of people milling about in front of the **Laima Clock** (Laimas pulkstenis). This has been Riga's most popular meeting place since the clock bearing the name of the famous chocolate factory was erected in 1924.

To the left of the monument is **Bastion Hill** (Bastejkalns), a man-made mound created in the 19th century on a previously flat parcel of land with the earth of the archaic ramparts. Several winding paths lead to the top of the hill, from which there would be a great view were it not for the dozens of trees that surround it. Ornamental fragments of historic houses destroyed during World War II have been added to the park in several places. Scattered before and beyond the pedestrian bridge are five granite memorial stones bearing the names of people gunned down by Soviet troops in January 1991.

Statue of Mother Latvia at the Freedom Monument

On the right side of the Freedom Monument are the **National Opera House** ❿ (Latvijas Nacionālā opera; www.opera.lv) and gardens, the pride and joy of Riga. Once known as the German Theatre, it was the first building in Riga to be electrified, after a gas leak nearly destroyed the building. The tall smokestack next to the canal was a part of the power station that provided the energy to light the inside of the theatre and the surrounding neighbourhood – no mean feat in 1887. The nymph fountain and gardens were created the following year to celebrate the building's grand re-opening. Now home to the Riga opera and ballet companies, its opulent interior and stage, once graced by native sons Mikhail Baryshnikov and Boris Gudunov, are considered to be among Europe's greatest treasures.

On the opposite side of the canal is the **University of Latvia** (Latvijas Universitāte; www.lu.lv), which has been an institution of higher learning since 1869. The footbridge that crosses the canal was a posthumous gift from one of its professors, who in his will stipulated its construction so that students would have no excuse

The National Opera House

to be late for class. A nearby **Bergs Bazaar** (www.bergabazars.lv) is a stylish village-like enclave dating from 1887–1900, and one of Riga's premier shopping and dining destinations. Local boutiques offer both local and international items: hand-made chocolates, stylish clothing and furs, current and historical maps, beautiful soaps, Latvian linens, delectable pastries, French wine, and much more. On Saturdays there is an excellent Farmer's Market.

WÖHRMANN PARK

One of the oldest parks in Riga, **Wöhrmann Park** (Vērmanes dārzs) was created on a piece of land donated to the city by Anna G. Wöhrmann following its devastation. This was caused by the ill-advised torching of the suburbs in advance of an attack by Napoleon's troops in 1812 that never materialised. The kiosks located at the corners of the park and the main building date back to the 19th century when they were used as fruit stands and a mineral-water pavilion, respectively. It is still one of Riga's favourite patches of green and its benches are often crowded with young and old, while the renovated amphitheatre is usually occupied by dozens of Russian pensioners playing chess and chatting.

There are several sights and historic buildings worth seeing around the park. On Merķeļa you can see the façade of the **Latvian Society House** (Latviešu biedrības nams), decorated with an impressive art nouveau fresco. Painted by one of Latvia's finest artists, Janis Rozentāls, the fresco depicts ancient Latvian gods. The Latvian Society was instrumental in the creation of the Latvian state and it sponsored schools, seminars, literary works and choirs. In 1873, the Society also sponsored the first Latvian song festival. Further down the street is the **Riga Circus** (Rīgas cirks), the only permanent circus in the Baltics. Built in 1889, it was the first establishment to show silent films in Riga, and today it still fulfils its initial purpose of dazzling young and old with animal exhibitions and acrobatic performances.

On Barona you can visit the **Museum of Natural History** (Latvijas dabas muzejs; www.dabasmuzejs.gov.lv; Wed and Fri 10am–5pm, Thu until 7pm, Sat–Sun 11am–5pm), one of the oldest museums in the city. Inside are thousands of items ranging from the wonders of taxidermy to exotic butterflies and, for the more macabre, pickled body parts. The museum's rarest exhibit is a collection of fossilised fish dating back hundreds of millions of years.

It is also worth pausing while on Barona to see a museum dedicated to the man after whom the street was named. You can view the **Krišjānis Barons Museum** (Krišjāņa Barona memoriālais dzīvoklis; www.baronamuzejs.lv; Wed 1–7pm, Thu–Sun 11am–6pm) where the fabled collector of Latvian folk songs lived and worked for the last four years of his life. He died in 1923.

Chess in Wöhrmann Park

THE ESPLANADE

In the 18th century one of Riga's only natural hills covered the area that now comprises the **Esplanade Park** (Esplanāde). However, in 1784, following a devastating bombardment from this elevated position, it was decided to completely level the ancient mound. The sandy expanse was used at first by the military for training and parades, but was later transformed into a luscious park that hosted major events and fairs, including Riga's 700th anniversary celebrations in 1901.

Today the Esplanade is known for three monumental buildings, the most spectacular of which is the **Orthodox Cathedral** (Pareizticīgo katedrāle) completed in 1884. In an era when all other languages but Russian were officially suppressed, this church was to symbolise the power of the 'true faith' in the Baltics. Its five gilded cupolas and adjoining belfry no doubt made an impression just as they do today. Sadly, when the Soviets converted the building into a planetarium they destroyed many of the cathedral's frescoes, the work of the day's best artists. The cathedral has returned to its congregation after thorough renovation. Nearby on Brīvības Bulvāris 32, the **National History Museum of Latvia** (Latvijas Nacionālais vēstures muzejs; http://lnvm.lv; Tue–Sun 10am–5pm) affords the visitor an overview of the evolution of the Latvian nation from the Stone Age to the 19th century and beyond. Situated across the park on Valdemāra is the massive baroque-style building that is home to the **Latvian National Museum of Art** (Latvijas Nacionālais mākslas muzejs; www.lnmm.lv; Tue–Thu 10am–6pm, Fri until 8pm, Sat–Sun

⊙ LATVIAN FOLK SONGS

Latvians sing while they work, while they play, at sombre occasions and at celebrations. Apart from their language and love of nature, Latvians are most proud of their folk songs, called *dainas*, which have been passed down from one generation to the next. The songs embody the wisdom of their ancestors and expound on subjects as diverse as farming, religion, funeral rites and sex.

Among the earliest students of folk songs in Latvia was the German philosopher Johann Gotfried Herder (1744–1803), whose studies inspired his belief that a feeling of belonging to one's nation is one of the most basic of human needs. Eventually 19th-century Latvian intellectuals recognised the value of the *dainas* and began transcribing them, most notably Krišjānis Barons (1835–1923). He travelled around the countryside, often on foot, collecting these treasures and painstakingly recording them for posterity. He began publishing *dainas* in 1895 and by 1915 the collection had reached 217,996 songs. His work was continued long after his death and today the number of texts has swollen to nearly 1.2 million songs with nearly 30,000 melodies, one of the largest bodies of oral folklore in the world.

There are around 150 folk-song choirs in Latvia, and former president Vaira Vīķe-Freiberga is the author of two books on the subject, *Saules dainas* and *Linguistics and Poetics of Latvian Folk Songs*.

10am–5pm), built in 1905. Almost as interesting as the permanent exhibits of paintings by 18th-century Baltic German artists and the Latvian masters Rozentāls, Annuss, Valters, Padegs and Liberts, are the frescoes in the main hall of the building painted by the nation's most revered artist, Vilhelms Purvītis. Standing outside the museum is a **statue of Janis Rozentāls** (1866–1916), whose painting *Leaving the Cemetery* is displayed inside and should not be missed.

Not far from the National Art Museum is the ivy-clad, brick neo-Gothic **Latvian Academy of Art** (Latvijas Mākslas akadēmija), also built in 1905.

Located just off the park on Skolas is **Jews in Latvia** (Ebreji Latvijā; www.jewishmuseum.lv; Sun–Thu 11am–5pm, May–Sept also Fri; donations expected), a museum dedicated to the achievements of the Latvian Jewish community, its destruction during the Nazi occupation during World War II, and its revival after the war and regaining of independence in 1991.

Madonna with a Machine Gun, by Kārlis Padegs

ART NOUVEAU DISTRICT ⬤

The whole of the city centre can be described as an art nouveau gallery, with one in three buildings in this flamboyant style, but Elizabetes, Antonijas, Strēlnieku, Vīlandes and, especially, Albert Street have been particularly blessed with this optimistic form of architecture. Two factors have led to this phenomenon. Riga's wealth was at its zenith at the end of the 19th century and the years preceding World War I, which happened to coincide with the popularity of this expressive art style. And, although hundreds of German cities also had an abundance of these buildings, many were completely

Father and son

The architect and engineer Mikhail Eisenstein (1867–1921), who is responsible for some of the city's most beautiful art nouveau buildings, is also known for being the father of the famous Russian filmmaker Sergei Eisenstein (*Battleship Potemkin*), who was born in Riga in 1898.

destroyed during World War II, yet most of Riga's art nouveau gems miraculously survived invasions by both Nazis and Soviets.

Start your tour at No. 33 Elizabetes, the beige building designed by Mikhail Eisenstein (1867–1921) that looks like an elaborate wedding cake. Across the street at No. 10b is perhaps his most well-known work, easily recognised by the incredibly long human faces on either side of a peacock – the symbol of art nouveau. Next door at No. 10a is yet another of the architect's buildings that displays hints of Biological Romanticism and some of the most bizarrely shaped windows in the city. Proceed to **Albert Street** Ⓜ (Alberta iela) where nearly all of the buildings are not only art nouveau, but also designed by Eisenstein. On the corner of Alberta and Strēlnieku in what used to be the house of the Latvian architect Konstantīns Pēkšēns is the Riga Art Nouveau Museum (Rīgas Jūgendstila muzejs, www.jugendstils.riga.lv; Tue–Sun 10am–6pm).

At the far end of Alberta street is the **Museum of Janis Rozentāls and Rūdolfs Blaumanis** (Jaņa Rozentāla un Rūdolfa Blaumaņa muzejs; http://memorialiemuzeji.lv; Wed–Sun

11am–6pm), the building in which the painter Rozentāls (1866–1916) and the playwright Blaumanis once lived and worked. Even if these Latvian cultural icons have no meaning for you, it's worth looking inside at the elaborate art nouveau staircase and interior. There are several other noteworthy buildings of this style two blocks over on Vīlandes.

MOSCOW DISTRICT

For centuries, ethnic Russians have inhabited this district of Riga, known locally as 'Little Moscow'. Among the oldest of its communities are the Old Believers, a religious group that fled to the area in the late 17th century to escape persecution in Russia. The area beyond the five pavilions of the Central Market was also a vibrant

10b Elizabetes, by Mikhail Eisenstein

centre of Riga's Jewish life, which was brutally extinguished under the Nazis. Unlike the orderly German-influenced streets and manicured parks of the city centre, the **Moscow District** (Maskavas Forštate) always had a wild streak and character all its own. Its 19th-century wooden houses and art nouveau buildings have yet to benefit from the city's economic boom, but the shopping malls, petrol stations, restaurants and exclusive car dealerships on the previously undeveloped land adjacent to Krasta Street are a testament to the area's potential value.

CENTRAL MARKET

The giant pavilions of the **Central Market** **N** (Centrāltirgus; www.rct.lv; daily 7am–6pm), used as zeppelin hangars during World War I, are located literally on the other side of the tracks and are one of the city's most exciting cultural treasures. When it was completed in 1930, it was one of the largest covered markets in Europe and to this day each of its four buildings still sells its originally intended products: fish, dairy, fruit and vegetables, and meat. The market spills out behind the main pavilions where you can buy anything from fake brand-name clothing to pirated music and software. Although it has become a tourist destination, many of its employees are not used to being photographed, so tread lightly and don't forget to hide your belongings from pickpockets. The warehouse quarter known as Spiķeri just beyond the Central Market on Maskavas street has become a trendy place full of cafes, bars, clubs and art galleries housed in renovated yellow brick buildings. At Maskavas 14a (entrance from Krasta st.) is the eye-opening Riga Ghetto and Latvian Holocaust Museum (Rīgas Geto muzejs; www.rgm.lv; Sun–Fri 10am–6pm) commemorating 70,000 Holocaust victims.

Further up Prāgas is the **Academy of Sciences** (Zinātņu akadēmija). Designed to glorify Stalin, its facade is littered

Stalinist architecture

with decorative hammers and sickles. Its 17th-floor observation deck gives great views of the city for a small charge. Behind this monument to communism is the wooden **Church of Jesus** (Jēzus baznīca), built in 1822 to replace an earlier house of worship destroyed in the fire that consumed Riga's suburbs a decade earlier. Its unusual octagonal shape was designed to fit the square's limited space.

At the corner of Gogoļa and Dzirnavu streets are the reconstructed ruins of the **Great Choral Synagogue** (Die Greise Hor Shul), which was set ablaze on 4 July 1941 with hundreds of Jewish Lithuanian refugees inside. A memorial stone and a menorah mark the spot of the atrocity. The area around Ludzas iela was part of a ghetto created by the Nazis.

THE LEFT BANK

The left bank (Pārdaugava) of the River Daugava is home to both apartment blocks and heavy industry. Its working-class neighbourhoods are full of renovated historic 19th-century wooden houses, charming churches, decaying art nouveau masterpieces and ultra-modern buildings, including the sleek National Library of Latvia (www.lnb.lv; guided tours on request) resembling a glass hill Also known as

the Castle of Light, it was designed by the famous Latvian architect Gunārs Birkerts.

RAILWAY AND AVIATION MUSEUMS

The building that houses the **Latvian Railway History Museum** (Latvijas dzelzceļa muzejs; www.railwaymuseum.lv; Tue–Wed, Fri–Sat 10am–5pm, Thu until 8pm) was a repair workshop for trains in the 19th century. Today it contains a variety of exhibits, from engineers' overalls and black-and-white photographs to old wagons and tools used by railway workers. Locomotives and historic carriages on the tracks outside will impress trainspotters. The museum has also become a popular venue for concerts.

On exiting the airport terminal go left towards the cargo buildings to find the **Riga Aviation Museum** (Rīgas aviācijas muzejs; http://airmuseum.lv; Mon–Fri 10am–4pm, Sat–Sun by appointment only). Cold War historians and spy novel enthusiasts shouldn't pass up an opportunity to acquaint themselves with the rusting examples of some of the Soviet Union's finest and, in some cases, most unusual aircraft.

VICTORY PARK

Just over the river is a park with a controversial monument dedicated to the victory over Nazi Germany and the so-called 'liberation' of Latvia. **Victory Park** (Uzvaras parks) is still a popular rallying point for leftists and pensioners on important Soviet anniversary days, yet Latvians view it as a symbol of the loss of their sovereignty and the occupation of their nation by a foreign power. Indeed, a small group of ultranationalists even tried to liberate Riga from its presence with sticks of dynamite. They were unsuccessful. Below the soaring pedestal that supports golden communist stars, Russian-speaking couples lay flowers on their wedding day.

Latvian Song and Dance Festival

OUTLYING AREAS

Once you leave Old Riga and the city centre, the sites worth seeing become fewer and farther between, but the following buildings, parks, museums and monuments are all worth the effort and the inexpensive tram, trolleybus or cab ride.

INTERESTING CEMETERIES

Construction of **Brothers' Cemetery** (Brāļu kapi), dedicated to Latvia's fallen heroes who fought for independence between 1915 and 1920, began in 1924 and was completed in 1936. Among its most impressive features are the sombre statues of soldiers, heads bowed, the eternal flame and Mother Latvia overseeing the entire scene. Take tram route number 11 from Barona.

    There are a few other interesting cemeteries worth visiting along the way. The **Great Cemetery** (Lielie kapi) was

opened in the late 18th century and contains the graves of Krišjānis Barons and other famous Latvians. Sadly, most of its artistically significant monuments were shipped to other parts of the USSR after the war to be used by the families of Soviet functionaries. Just across the street next to the tiny Orthodox church is the **Pokrov Cemetery** (Pokrova kapi) with gravestones bearing the epitaphs of prominent tsarist bureaucrats. A small plot of land is also dedicated to Red Army soldiers who were killed in the area during World War II. Further along the tram route is the city's largest final resting place, the **Forest Cemetery** (Meža kapi), which is still used today.

☉ MIDSUMMER CELEBRATIONS

While Christmas and Easter often top the list of favourite national holidays for many countries, Midsummer's Eve is the most anticipated celebration of the year in Latvia. This ancient pagan fertility festival marks the longest day of the year and its passing is observed across the country on 23–24 June. All of the nation's urban centres empty as cars decorated with oak leaves head for the countryside laden with food and drink. Rural hosts greet their guests with beer, caraway-seed cheese and a song, but the new arrivals aren't able to join the fun until they sing something in return. During the course of the evening, young couples are encouraged to forage through the forest for the fabled fern flower that only blooms on Midsummer. Of course, ferns don't blossom, but it's a charming euphemism for the fertility part of the festivities. Revellers also jump over the bonfire three times for good luck and no one is allowed to sleep until sunrise.

The Ethnographic Open-Air Museum

FOREST PARK (MEŽAPARKS)

By the late 19th century, Riga's elite had had enough of the city's overcrowded streets and decided to create a park far from the noise and grime of the centre where they could relax in the bosom of nature. Kaiser Park, as it was originally known, was one of Europe's first garden cities, where only summer cottages and entertainment complexes were allowed to be built. Many of those magnificent wooden houses have now been restored and this green section of Riga now commands the city's highest real estate prices.

Forest Park is also home to the **Song Festival Grounds** (Lielā estrāde) where tens of thousands of performers and spectators gather every five years for this monumental undertaking. The **Riga National Zoo** (Rīgas zooloģiskais dārzs; http://riga zoo.lv; Apr–Oct 10am–7pm, Nov–Mar 10am–5pm) is another great reason to visit.

THE ETHNOGRAPHIC OPEN-AIR MUSEUM OF LATVIA

A 20-minute trip on Bus No. 1 from Tērbatas will transport you to the rural countryside of 19th-century Latvia. Explore more than 100 hectares (247 acres) of life as it used to be in peasant villages and seaside fishing communities. Established in 1924, the **Ethnographic Open-Air Museum of Latvia ❶** (Latvijas etnogrāfiskais brīvdabas muzejs; www.brivdabasmuzejs.lv; daily 10am–5pm, in summer grounds until 8pm) is one of the oldest of its kind in Europe and also one of the most impressive. Its architects scoured the agrarian landscape of the nation in search of priceless examples of typical wooden homes, barns, stables, shops, churches and windmills and had them taken apart and painstakingly reassembled here on the shores of Lake Jugla. Weavers, blacksmiths, beekeepers and various craftsmen go about their business here in authentic costumes and sell their wares to the delight of all who come. During the summer a variety of folklore concerts and craft markets are held here, as well as Midsummer's Eve celebrations (see page 67).

RIGA MOTOR MUSEUM

In the wilds of nine-storey Soviet concrete housing estates in the suburbs, you can view the country's best display of antique cars, motorcycles and military vehicles at the **Riga Motor Museum** (Rīgas motormuzejs; www.motormuzejs.lv; daily 10am–6pm). Vintage Rolls Royces are lined up next to BMWs and Mercedes, not to mention Latvian automobiles produced in the 1920s and 1930s. Among the museum's most impressive exhibits are the cars used by the Soviet elite, including specially designed limousines.

SALASPILS CONCENTRATION CAMP MEMORIAL

Just outside Riga city limits is the sleepy town of Salaspils, which has the dubious distinction of being the scene of one of the 20th

The popular beach at Jūrmala

century's most barbaric crimes against humanity. Hidden beyond the pines of its forest is the site of a former Nazi concentration camp, 'Kurtenhof', where more than 100,000 Jews, Latvians, Estonians, Lithuanians, Poles and nearly a dozen other ethnic groups were exterminated. A megalithic concrete structure, which now serves as the gate to the camp and also houses a small exhibit dedicated to the site, is inscribed with the words, 'Beyond this gate the earth moans'. Visitors can view the foundations of some of the prisoners' barracks and the sad sculptures symbolising the suffering of the camp's victims.

DAY TRIPS

The proud inhabitants of the countryside will be the first people to tell you that Riga isn't Latvia. Away from the luxury cars, trendy cafés and designer shops of the city that supports over a third of the nation's population are several historic towns that have yet to shed their traditional lifestyles for the trappings of modern cosmopolitan living. Ancient crusader castles, health spas, over 500km (310 miles) of pristine beaches, and hundreds of nature trails for hikers are only a short day trip from the capital city. All of the following destinations are easily accessible by hired car, public transport or organised tour.

JŪRMALA

This loose federation of a dozen small towns spread over nearly 20km (12 miles) of white-sand beaches has long been a favourite summer retreat for Riga's citizens. From its inception as a holiday destination in the 19th century, when bathing hours for men and women were strictly regulated to prevent the unseemly commingling of the sexes, to its heyday in the 1930s, when seasonal cottages were built nearly every day, **Jūrmala ❷**, with little more than its beauty and proximity to the sea, has never lost its allure. In fact, during the Soviet era this narrow peninsula jutting out into the Baltic became one of the USSR's most popular resorts, enticing more than 6 million hard-working proletarians to its shores each year. However, this boom time, in which development went largely unregulated, left parts of this unique landscape scarred with crumbling communist edifices. Many of the current entrepreneurs in the area have also failed to shed their old mindset, so service can often fall short of Western expectations.

But Jūrmala's draw has always been its excellent beaches sheltered by pine forests and sand dunes. In recent years standards have improved so dramatically as to warrant the prestigious European blue flags that guarantee essential services such as sanitation, changing rooms, lifeguards and medical teams on call. Beer gardens have also sprouted up like mushrooms to meet the demands of thirsty holidaymakers. During the few hot summer months that Latvia experiences, you can expect beaches teeming with people sunbathing, playing football and parading the body beautiful.

Jūrmala is also home to dozens of spa hotels that offer mud baths and scores of other health treatments often used by German and Finnish pensioners who can't afford such luxuries in their own countries. The urban centres provide top-notch restaurants and nightlife as well as excellent

⊘ LAND OF STORKS

If babies come from storks, where to do storks come from? The answer is Latvia. While the number of storks in Europe on the whole is in steady decline, their numbers in Latvia have increased dramatically. Many nations in Western Europe and Scandinavia are now completely lacking in these noble birds, but Latvia has nearly 10,000 pairs of nesting storks, or one pair for every 250 people.

Latvia is also home to the rare black stork, which, unlike its white cousin that often chooses chimneys as nesting platforms, is very shy and only nests in uninhabited areas of the countryside. If the black stork detects the presence of humans, it often abandons its nest.

Latvians have always revered storks and they encourage these large birds to nest on their property by erecting special poles for their huge nests, which often reach 1m (3ft) in diameter. The birds are thought to bring luck, to protect the home and bring fertility. Just drive out of Riga's city limits in nearly any direction in the summer and you're likely to see them. The storks then head back to Africa before the harsh Latvian winter arrives.

examples of wooden art nouveau buildings, not least of which is the **Dubulti Lutheran Church** (Dubultu luterāņu baznīca), whose towering steeple can be seen from a great distance. Those interested in literature can visit the **Rainis and Aspazija Memorial Summer Cottage** (Raiņa un Aspazijas vasarnīca; http://memorialiemuzeji.lv; Tue–Sat 10am–5pm) and see where two of Latvia's most famous writers lived and worked. The library has a collection of more than 7,000 books in 11 languages. A casual stroll down the main pedestrian street of Jomas iela in Majori will afford every visitor with countless opportunities to eat, drink and shop.

One of Latvia's best nature reserves is located at the far west end of Jūrmala. **Ķemeri National Park** (Ķemeru Nacionālais parks) has wetlands, marshes, swamps and raised bogs that have all but disappeared in Western Europe. Nature trails and an observation tower allow visitors to explore the park's 43

Gutmanis Cave

Below the castle complex is a series of caves, including the largest in the Baltics, Gutmanis Cave (Gūtmaṇa ala), which measures nearly 19m (62ft) deep, 12m (40ft) wide and 10m (33ft) high. Because it is thought to be the place where the Turaida Rose met her end, lovers have left their inscriptions in its sandstone walls since the 17th century, many of which are still visible.

hectares (106 acres) and see a variety of animals, including wild boar, elk, deer, wolves and rare birds.

Trains depart for Jūrmala from Riga Central Station every half hour during the summer, and the trip to its largest town, Majori, takes 30–40 minutes.

SIGULDA

Liv tribesmen, who had settled in the Gauja River region around 1,000 years ago, built a wooden fortress high above the valley, but in 1207 it was destroyed by the Brotherhood of the Sword and replaced by a new stone castle. A small town, referred to by the crusaders as Siegewald, flourished at the foot of the new fortress and before long it included churches and even new castles. The fortunes of **Sigulda** ❸ changed when it was overrun twice by Russian troops in the Great Livonian War (1558–82), causing extensive damage. It suffered most, however, during the Polish–Swedish War (1600–29) when its fortifications were destroyed and the ensuing plague ravaged its population.

Sigulda did not recover until the 19th century with the opening of the Riga–Pskov railway. Its romantic castle ruins, ancient churches and picturesque valley soon became major tourist attractions earning its hilly, forest-covered terrain the nickname 'Latvia's Switzerland'. Today, Sigulda enjoys the country's most developed tourism infrastructure with the same proven sights, as well as new activities such as nature hikes on marked trails, rafting and canoeing trips on the river, rides down a bob-sleigh track and bungee jumping from a cable car above the valley. Sigulda is about an hour's ride by train from Riga.

Sigulda's most striking attraction is the **Turaida Museum Reserve** ❹ (Turaidas muzejrezervāts; www.turaida-muzejs.lv; daily May–Sept 9am–8pm, Oct until 7pm, Nov–Mar 10am–5pm), which offers several noteworthy historical sites, the most obvious being the partially reconstructed brick **Turaida Castle** (Turaidas pils), built in 1214. Archaeological excavations are continuing, but visitors can view the small museum dedicated to the castle and the Liv tribes that once lived in the area. The castle tower offers excellent views of the valley. Outside the castle grounds is one of the oldest wooden churches in Latvia, built in 1750.

View from Turaida Castle

Cable car in the Gauja valley

Next to the church, beside a giant linden tree, you can see the grave of Maija (1601–20), the **Turaida Rose** (Turaidas Roze). Legend has it that a clerk who lived in the castle discovered a young girl on a battlefield among the dead and dying. She grew up to become a beautiful woman and, despite the interest displayed by the local gentry, fell in love with a commoner who tended the castle gardens. A Polish soldier was entirely enamoured with the girl and asked her hand in marriage, but she refused. Furious, the man and another soldier lured her to a nearby cave and attempted to rape her. To protect her virtue, she offered the man a gift of a scarf that could supposedly protect its wearer from harm. As proof of its magical qualities she asked the soldier to try to cut her with his sword. To his horror, the dim-witted man lopped her head off. Today, newlyweds leave flowers at her grave in the hope of attaining the same everlasting love. Curiously, medieval records were found that included an account of a woman named Maija who was murdered in the Gutmanis Cave, which may prove that the legend is at least partially based on fact.

Beyond the grave is **Folk Song Hill** (Dainu kalns), which is essentially a sculpture park with figures representing various aspects of Latvian folklore and mythology.

Not far from the cable car that leads to the Sigulda city centre are the ruins of the **Krimulda Castle** (Krimuldas pils). Not much remains of the fortress, built in 1312, and it is seldom seen by tourists, but it's worth a visit, especially if you have time to spare while waiting for the next cable car.

The **Sigulda Castle** ❺ (Siguldas pils) is located on the other side of the valley. Its most impressive features apart from its location are the tower of the grand gate and the Gothic windows of the chapel. Sigulda's first castle was abandoned after its destruction in the 17th century, but a new **manor house** was built next to it, which now houses the city council and a restaurant. All 1.2km (3⁄4 mile) of the **Sigulda Bobsleigh Track** (Siguldas bobslejtrase; www.bob trase.lv; daily 8am–8pm) are located next to the railway station and guarantee a unique experience for anyone brave enough to take a ride down.

Bauska Castle

BAUSKA REGION

Although the town of Bauska has little to offer apart from its impressive castle ruins, two magnificent palaces are located within 10km (6 miles) of the city and all three attractions can be incorporated into a day trip from Riga.

Construction of **Bauska Castle** (Bauskas pils; www.bauskaspils. lv; May–Sept daily 9am–7pm, Oct daily until 6pm, Nov–Apr Tue–Sun 11am–5pm) began in 1443 as yet another fortress of the Livonian Order. Later it became the residence of the royal family of the Duchy of Courland. Built on a hill above the confluence of two rivers, its ramparts, deep moat, five towers and 4m (13ft) thick walls were still not enough to prevent its partial destruction during the Great Northern War (1700–21) between Russia and Sweden. Today its well-preserved ruins are no less impressive. Inside are a small museum and an observation tower.

The German barons left behind hundreds of manors and estates across Latvia, but none as grand as **Rundāle Palace** ❻ (Rundāles pils; http://rundale.net; May–Oct 10am–6pm, Nov–Apr until 5pm). Latvia's most opulent building was the brainchild of Bartolomeo Rastrelli (1700–71), who would later design the Winter Palace in St Petersburg, one-time residence of the tsars and current home of the Hermitage Museum. Rundāle Palace was built between 1736 and 1740, as a residence for Duke Ernst Johann von Biron of Courland (1690–1772). The duke was a favourite of Tsarina Anna (1693–1740), but was stripped of his title on her death, only to return in 1765 after Catherine the Great assumed the throne of Russia. The palace is the best example of baroque architecture in Latvia and, although it suffered during the wars that ravaged the region, many of its finest attributes have survived. After being issued felt slippers to avoid disturbing the delicate parquet floors, visitors can view a few of the original 138 rooms, including the Gold and White Representation Halls, the Duchess' Boudoir

Rundāle Palace

and the Duke's apartments. An exhibit featuring European and Oriental art and other historic treasures is open to the public, as is the French garden and an exhibit dedicated to priceless religious artefacts saved by Latvians from imminent destruction at the hands of the Soviets.

Mežotne Palace (Mežotnes pils; www.mezotnepalace.com; daily 10am–4pm) has been completely renovated and is currently used as a hotel, although it is open to the public for tours. It was completed in 1802 and used to belong to Charlotte von Lieven, a close friend of Catherine the Great. Unfortunately the palace was gutted several times by various invading troops. The graves in the English garden of seven Russian soldiers who held off a German assault here in 1915, bear witness to this violent history. Its location on the River Lielupe makes it a great place for a picnic, but those who would prefer to live like royalty can rent a room in the palace and soak up the neoclassical atmosphere first-hand.

The opulent Opera House

WHAT TO DO

Riga has no shortage of things to do. Get lost among the amber stalls of Old Riga or take in a world-class ballet performance at the city's beautifully restored 19th-century opera house. Duck into a dark club for a taste of whisky and the delta blues or join the crowds at a summer beer garden and order a local brew. Whatever your pleasure, Riga has something for everyone, including the kids.

ENTERTAINMENT

With more than a million folk songs to choose from, Latvians are never short of words to sing, and their collective voice for recent independence was dubbed 'The Singing Revolution'. Similarly, locals have the utmost respect for all things musical, and the result is a vibrant cultural scene. Riga is, after all, the birthplace of classical musician Gidon Kremer, actor and choreographer Mikhail Baryshnikov and film director Sergei Eisenstein.

CLASSICAL MUSIC AND OPERA

With such native sons as Baryshnikov and Alexander Gudunov, it's no surprise that Riga's ballet and opera draw crowds from around Europe. However, what's most

Song and dance

The Latvian Song and Dance Festival has been held roughly every five years since 1873 and its highlight is the final concert during which hundreds of choirs from around the country sing together in front of tens of thousands of spectators who often join in on the most popular songs. They take place approximately every five years – the next one is scheduled for 2023.

surprising to visitors are the low prices for performances and the stunning opulence of the **National Opera House** (Aspazijas bulvāris 3; tel: 6707 37 77; www.opera.lv), which is decorated with gilded ceilings, crystal chandeliers and priceless works of art. The **Great Guild** (Amatu 6; www.lnso.lv) is home to the Latvian Philharmonic Orchestra, while the **Small Guild** (Amatu 3/5; tel: 6703 74 18 or 6722 37 72; http://mazagilde.lv) across the street often hosts chamber music concerts and special events. No trip to Riga is complete without experiencing an organ concert in the Baltic's largest house of worship, **Dome Cathedral** (Doma lau-kums 1; tel: 6721 32 13; www.doms.lv). Professionals from around the globe often waive their charges just to play on the magnificent organ, which is one of the world's largest, with 6,718 pipes. Most major rock and pop concerts are held at **Arena Riga** (Skanstes 21; www.arenariga.com).

NIGHTLIFE

The best feature of having fun in a northern city such as Riga is the extreme daylight hours; in summer, the sun doesn't set until very late, so you're not easily tempted to head back to your hotel, and in winter it's so dark that you don't need an excuse to begin early. But geography and seasonal anomalies aren't the only things the Latvian capital has in its favour. Trendy cocktail bars, chic clubs, 24-hour casinos and down-to-earth pubs occupy nearly every street corner in Riga and they are all now smoke-free as the law requires smokers to light up outside or in designated, well-ventilated smoking areas.

For a cosy, dimly lit atmosphere and expertly poured mixed drinks with Rīgas Melnais Balzams, the potent national elixir (see page 86), take the steps down to the cellar of **Balzambārs** (Torņa 4; tel: 6721 44 94; www.balzambars.lv). A popular **B-Bar** located next to the Dome Cathedral (Doma laukums 2; www.bbars.lv), it purportedly offers the best drinks in town. For live jazz music visit **Riga Jazz Club** (Palasta iela 10; tel: 2944 05 88), but those out for a more local experience should take in a concert by a Latvian band at **Četri Balti Krekli** (Vecpilsētas 12; www.krekli.lv). For dancing and seeing how the young and fashionable dress, try the popular club **Coyote Fly** (Tērbatas

Summer evenings are perfect for al fresco entertainment

ielā 2, www.coyotefly.lv) featuring the best Latvian DJs and VJs or nearby fashionable **Studio 69** (Tērbatas iela 73, tel: 6750 60 30; http://info.studio69.lv). The **Royal Casino** (www.royalcasino.lv) is a huge spa, hotel, restaurant and casino complex open 24 hours; Latvian law requires that you register your passport at the door.

SHOPPING

In Riga you can buy nearly anything available in other major European cities, from designer clothes and jewellery to brand-name jeans and trainers.

Competition is fierce, and empty storefronts are a testament to the volatile nature of commerce in Riga. Handicrafts and food products such as sweets are among the best goods produced in Latvia, and they are often inexpensive and make excellent souvenirs and gifts. Most shops accept major credit cards, but look for stickers at the entrance or on the cash register to be sure.

WHERE TO SHOP

There is no specific shopping district in Riga. Most souvenir and local handicraft shops as well as art galleries can be found in the old city and what seems an endless queue of amber stalls awaits you on Līvu Square, Skārņu and Vaļņu iela. Haggling is seldom required and will probably be frowned upon, as most prices are fairly universal. Fashion and electronics are more commonly found in the city centre, especially on K. Barona, Brīvības and Tērbatas streets. Antiques shops can be found all over the city and usually specialise in porcelain, paintings, icons and a variety of memorabilia from the Soviet era.

Amber stalls

Even if you don't want to spend any money, the Central Market (see page 63) is well worth a visit. Dairy, meat, fresh produce and seafood are sold in four of the five pavilions that once served as zeppelin hangars during World War I. Improvements in hygiene apart, you will be treated to a colourful scene that has remained largely unchanged since the market first opened in the 1930s. Rotund women entice shoppers with taunting remarks and examples of their best cuts of meat or samples of fresh cheese or yoghurt as men with arms like tree trunks skilfully dissect livestock and display the butchered beasts' prime cuts. The stalls spill out onto the pavement behind the buildings where anything from cheap garments to CDs are sold.

WHAT TO BUY

Since ancient times, the polished chunks of petrified tree sap that wash up on the shores of the Baltic Sea have been a useful commodity to the region's inhabitants and their diverse trading partners. **Amber** is still the most popular souvenir bought in Latvia and is sold in every souvenir shop or outdoor stall. It comes in various sizes, in colours ranging from light yellow to dark brown and can even be found with prehistoric flora and insects trapped inside. Avoid the shady amber touts who present their dubious wares from a plastic bag. **Silver** rings, bracelets and earrings based on ancient Baltic designs and motifs are also popular examples of local decorative jewellery. The braided, rope-like ring worn by most Latvians is called a *Nameja gredzens*. It symbolises national unity and is named after a famous 13th-century tribal chieftain who refused to submit to the invading German crusaders.

Many traditional Latvian handicrafts also make practical gifts or souvenirs and can often be a unique addition to your home's interior design. Latvia is famous for its **linen** products, most notably tablecloths, which are available in many different styles, some with simple Latvian symbols and patterns, others dyed in various colours for more modern tastes. Hand-woven **blankets** coloured with only natural dyes, hand-carved **wooden toys**, wicker baskets

Let's go Latvia!

Sports enthusiasts and those who would prefer a memento of Latvia's more recent history can buy national hockey or football team jerseys or scarves embroidered with the local battle cry, *Sarauj Latvija!*, which can be loosely translated as 'Let's go, Latvia!'

and stunning glazed **ceramics** are also on offer at most souvenir shops. An excellent place to buy Latvian crafts, fashion by local designers as well as food and drink is the bustling Kalnciema fair held at the corner of Melnsila and Kalnciema streets every Saturday from 10am–4pm.

Riga's **antiques shops** usually offer an eclectic collection of knick-knacks, porcelain statues and tableware, paintings and furniture. Many also specialise in Russian religious icons, but one should bear in mind that an icon's journey from a local chapel to a shop may not have been sanctioned by its parishioners or the government. Ask for documentation if the icon's history is unclear. Soviet memorabilia, including uniforms, medals, coins and busts of Lenin, are also widely available,

⊙ MEDICINAL PURPOSES

Rīgas Melnais Balzams or Riga Black Balsam is perhaps one of the best souvenirs you can buy in Latvia. It has been produced in Latvia since 1752 when a pharmacist began marketing his concoction of 25 herbs, flowers, berries and other secret ingredients as an elixir. Given the fact that it also has an alcohol content of 45 percent and contains wormwood, the substance that gives absinthe its kick, it's no wonder that people forgot about their pain, at least for an hour or two. Bottled in brown ceramic jugs, it's also an attractive gift to inflict on your friends. Although Latvians still drink the black bitter neat, especially as a hangover cure, most locals combine it with coffee, cola or fruit juice. Hot blackcurrant nectar with a shot of Balzams is one of Riga's most popular winter cocktails, although some prefer the Riga Souvenir – Balzams mixed with local sparkling wine. Enjoy the national drink at your own risk.

Colourful local knits

as are silver spoons from tsarist times. Tourists are also often surprised by the amount of antique books that are available in German and Russian – the languages of the old empire.

Music always makes a good gift and Riga's pedigree as home to Richard Wagner and Eurovision superstar band Brainstorm (Prāta Vētra) is reason enough to buy a local CD. The Latvian Folk Music Collection series produced by the Upe Recording Studio is a good place to start. Each CD in the series is based on a theme such as Latvian dances, songs about war, and songs about beer. The disc of Latvian lullabies is a perfect present for parents with small children. Albums by Skandinieki and Iļģi are also recommended. Recordings of the song festival held every five years (see page 81), and of organ concerts at the Dome Cathedral, are also good choices.

Finally, what better way to remember your trip, than to bring **local food** back home? Laima chocolates have been made in Riga since the early 20th century and are simply delicious, not to mention cheap. Black and rye breads are baked according to traditional recipes and never use food colouring to achieve their golden brown hues. Latvians judge honey the way the French judge a good wine, and prices vary widely depending on what flowers the bees visited to collect their pollen. Caraway-seed cheese served at Midsummer festivities is as Latvian a food as they come, but is not everyone's cup of tea, so you may wish to taste a free sample at the market before buying a large quantity. Definitely an acquired taste are miniature lamprey eels cooked in their own juices and then tinned for export. Germans and Latvians love them, and perhaps you will, too.

SPORTS

Latvians love sports, and not just the ones that they're good at. You'll often find as many locals as expatriates watching English Premiership football at sports bars and your average male can usually spout off enough statistics about his favourite Formula 1 driver to make you wonder if he has a vested interest in Williams or Ferrari.

Ice hockey is a national obsession and Latvians worship their hip-checking heroes, especially the ones that play in the NHL. Each year at the beginning of May businesses close early and the citizens of Riga head out to their favourite pubs to watch their team strive for glory in the World Hockey Championship. A victory often leads to gatherings of hundreds of fans who parade about the city shouting slogans and singing songs, often ending their wanderings at the embassy of their vanquished foes. A new arena was built for the hockey championship in 2006, when the Soviet-style Rīgas Sporta Pils was finally retired. In 2007, the Russian Super Hockey League was replaced by the Kontinental Hockey League, which includes a few teams like Dynamo Riga (www.dinamoriga.lv), located beyond the borders of the Russian Federation. Home games are played at Arena Riga. Although it doesn't command the same amount of respect

Bobsleigh run at Sigulda

that hockey does, **football** has become increasingly popular, especially since Latvia participated in the Euro 2004 Football Championship in Portugal where they held world-champions Germany to a draw. After winning the Latvian Championship every year since the club's founding in 1991, FC Skonto were finally dislodged from their exalted position in 2005. The team recovered the title in 2010 and finished as runner-up in 2015. However, the club regrettably went bankrupt in 2016. FC Skonto matches in Riga used to be held at the Skonto Stadium (E. Melngaiļa 1a, www.skontofc.com), which is now the Riga FC club home ground. Riga FC was founded in 2014 and in 2018 it became the Latvian Higher League champion.

The only other sports that have met with any success involve helmets, skin-tight suits, a lot of ice and a steep incline. The historic town of Sigulda, just a short ride from Riga (see page

74), has the only world-class **bobsleigh and luge run** (www.
bobtrase.lv) in the former Soviet Union. When professionals
aren't training at the difficult run on weekends, an instructor
will take you for a quick slide down the mountain year-round
at speeds in excess of 125kmh (80mph).

If a relaxing round of **golf** is more to your liking, you can
choose from an exclusive 18-hole lakeside course (OZO,
Mielgrāvja 16; tel: 6739 43 99; www.ozogolf.lv) owned by the
hockey star Sandis Ozoliņš, Jūrmala Golf Club & Hotel (Golfa
iela 1, Pinki; tel: 6716 03 00; http://jgch.lv), which opened
in 2018 and offers an 18-hole course, or a less challenging
nine-hole course by the airport (Viesturi; tel: 2644 43 90;
www.golfsviesturi.lv).

CHILDREN

There are only so many churches and historic art nouveau
buildings that a child can bear before throwing a tantrum. Riga
may not be the most child-friendly city in Eastern Europe, but
a growing number of restaurateurs have become aware of the
problem and have invested in high chairs for their younger
customers. Vairāk Saules (Dzirnavu 60; tel: 6728 28 78; www.
vairaksaules.lv) offers a play area for the kids to get lost in
and T.G.I. Friday's (Kaļku 6; tel: 6722 90 71; http://lat.fridays.
lv) provides a kids' menu and colouring books.

The state **Puppet Theatre** (K. Barona 16/18; tel: 6728 53 55;
www.lelluteatris.lv) is an excellent place for children to spend
time with one another and, although the plays are performed in
either Latvian or Russian, the plot is generally easy enough to
follow and is seldom as interesting as the puppets themselves.

Laima Chocolate Musuem (Miera 22, tel: 6615 47 77; www.lai
masokoladesmuzejs.lv; closed Mon). The tour of Latvia's oldest

chocolate and sweets factory includes workshops (advance booking essential) where children can learn how to make chocolate, get plenty of treats and have a picture beside the famous Laima clock – the symbol of love, joy and new beginnings.

The **Latvian Open-Air Ethnographic Museum** (Brīvības gatve 440; tel: 6799 45 15; see page 69) provides 100 hectares (247 acres) of life the way it used to be where children and adults can learn about rural peasant life during the 19th century. Blacksmiths operate the bellows and forge horseshoes and other iron souvenirs, beekeepers extract honey for tourists to taste, and horse-riding can also be arranged. The **Museum of Natural History** (see page 57) is also a good option for children and indeed many school groups often wander its hallways. Ancient fossils, mounted taxidermic wonders, and all manner of creepy-crawly insects are on display for any curious child to admire.

At the **Zinoo Science and Curiosity Center** (Dzirnavu 67, Gallerija Rīga) 5th floor; tel: 2839 16 69; www.zinoo.lv) the interactive exhibits encourage children to explore the secrets of science with the slanting room, Tesla coil or levitating water being major attractions.

The **Riga National Zoo** (see page 68) is also a logical choice for children and the young at heart. Recent improvements

Bear at Riga Zoo

Lido Leisure Centre

have made the Soviet-era exhibitions much more palatable to the Western tourist. A quick tram ride from the centre will bring you in sight of lions, leopards, musk oxen, alligators and other beasts from around the globe.

Although not quite what P.T. Barnum envisioned, the **Riga Circus** (Merķeļa 4; tel: 6721 34 79; www.cirks.lv) is also a good place to view animals; it has been in operation for over 100 years so it must be doing something right. The circus is seasonal and is closed each year from Easter until the third Friday in October.

Līvu Akvaparks **water park** (Lielupe, Vienības gatve 36; tel: 6775 56 36; www.akvaparks.lv) offers six water slides, a wave pool, children's pool, a tubing river and various other attractions guaranteed to keep the kids engaged for several hours. The 'Tornado" tube is one of the biggest in the world.

No trip to Riga would be complete without a short trip to the kitschy **Lido Leisure Centre** (Krasta 76; tel: 6770 00 00; www.lido.lv). The complex's main attraction is a huge log cabin, which offers three floors of Latvian restaurants and beer halls with live music and a supervised children's room with interactive games, colouring books and other activities. Outside is an **amusement park**, which offers slides, games, pony rides, in-line skating and ice-skating in winter.

CALENDAR OF EVENTS

Riga is never short of concerts and festivals, but organisers seldom know exact dates until shortly before an event. Opera schedules are among the most reliable and can be found at www.opera.lv. For an up-to-date events schedule try *Riga In Your Pocket*, available at kiosks and bookshops around town. See also page 129 for a list of public holidays.

February–March The International Bach Chamber Music festival (www.music.lv) draws musicians from all over Europe.

April The International Baltic Ballet Festival (www.ballet-festival.lv) is held each year and features the best performers from the Baltic Sea region.

June An annual crafts fair is held at the Ethnographic Museum on the first weekend of the month.

22 June Annual Dome Square crafts fair.

23–24 June Midsummer's Eve. Latvia's favourite national holiday is celebrated on the actual date and never moved to the closest weekend for the sake of convenience. The pagan fertility celebrations consist of singing, dancing, lots of beer and bonfires in the countryside.

June Riga Opera Festival. The annual festival takes place annually for roughly two weeks and celebrities have included Warren Mok, Inese Galante and other international stars (www.opera.lv).

July *Rīgas Ritmi* Rhythmic Music Festival. Contemporary jazz stars (international and domestic) take part in this annual festival (www.rigasritmi.lv), which now also has winter and spring concert sessions.

August–September Riga Sacred Music Festival (www.choirlatvija.lv). Each year musicians from around the Baltic and Europe converge on Riga to play religious music, especially at the Dome Cathedral. The annual autumn harvest festival is celebrated on the last Saturday of September in Old Riga.

September–October *Homo* Novus International Festival of Contemporary Theatre takes place annually in Riga. The festival started in 1995.

December Christmas concerts and crafts market on Dome Square.

EATING OUT

All of Latvia's invaders have left their mark on the nation's cuisine. A hodgepodge of different cultural influences, Latvian cuisine can best be summed up by listing its chief ingredients: pork, potatoes and cabbage. Most Latvians prefer their meals to be served without the benefit of universally accepted spices, but bland dishes are often enlivened with the crutches of national gastronomy, dill and caraway seeds. Menus have evolved since independence and, although nowhere near close to perfect, the standard of service has also improved dramatically.

Authentic ethnic restaurants have also mushroomed in the city, so that it's now possible to have sushi for lunch and dim sum for dinner. So many pizzerias have also opened in the city that pizza may well replace pork chops as the nation's food of choice. Although no longer objects of scorn, vegetarians should still be specific when ordering meals to ensure that a garden salad isn't topped with bacon or a supposedly meatless soup infused with chunks of ham.

The recent influx of foreign tourists has prompted local restaurant owners to raise the price of their meals considerably. That said, although you'll have to part with at least €10 for a steak, you can still find two-course lunch specials in the old town for roughly €6–8.

WHERE TO EAT

Many establishments in Riga try to be everything to everyone, often billing themselves as restaurants, clubs, bars and even casinos all in one, so the distinctions between them are often blurred. Some bars serve excellent food worthy of the finest gastronomic institutions in the city, and some restaurants are popular places simply to drink beer. The following is a general explanation of establishments you'll encounter in Riga.

Restorāni (restaurants) seem to occupy nearly every square metre of available space in Old Riga and some of the best areas of the centre. Although most restaurants have put their faith in international fare to ensure a diverse crowd of patrons, many have dedicated their kitchens to the creation of

Traditional grey peas with bacon and onions

delicious ethnic cuisines such as Indian, Armenian, Japanese and even Korean. If restaurant staff do not speak a foreign language apart from Russian, which will happen very rarely, menus are invariably written in English. Bear in mind that garnishes, bread and even condiments may not be included in the price of a meal and a 10 percent gratuity may be automatically added, so inspect the bill carefully before leaving a tip.

Locals often take comfort in their local *kafejnīcas* (cafés), which offer greasy dishes such as pork chops and other heavy foods guaranteed to clog your arteries. Prices are almost always just short of ridiculously cheap, but menus are rarely in English. Many of these establishments also offer an inexpensive buffet, so you can often just point to whatever you would like to eat.

Krogi (bars) usually offer menus for lunch and dinner and remain open for drinks until midnight and perhaps later, seldom closing before 2am on weekends. Most *alus bāri* (beer

Drinking etiquette

Always look each of your fellow drinkers in the eye when clinking beer mugs at a bar with locals. You can also impress Latvians by saying *priekā!*, which is Latvian for 'Cheers!'.

bars) are typically located around the railway station, central market and other areas that tend to attract unsavoury types who just can't do without a beer at 8 o'clock in the morning. Although a half-litre mug can cost as little as €2, the more tourist-friendly bars in the old town and the centre are a better choice for a pint.

WHEN TO EAT

Latvians eat a hearty meal for both lunch and dinner, usually at noon–2pm and 6pm–8pm, respectively. Although many bars serve food and are open until well after midnight, their kitchens usually close by 10pm. Breakfast is not a big event in Riga and, apart from major hotels, only a few restaurants offer eggs, bacon and sausages. Instead, at an average hotel you can expect a cold buffet of meat, cheese, cereals and coffee or tea.

WHAT TO EAT

Most Latvian menus are divided into the following categories: *aukstās uzkodas* (cold starters), *siltās uzkodas* (warm starters), *salāti* (salads), *zupas* (soups), *otrie ēdieni* (main courses), and *deserti* (desserts). Two- and three-course business lunches are also gaining in popularity and are invariably cheaper than ordering a meal *à la carte*.

Soups are a typical starter in Riga and, although menus differ, most places offer between three and five different choices. Cream of mushroom and pea and bacon soups are most common during the winter, while pink vegetarian borsch served cold is a summertime favourite. Fish such as salmon and herring are often served as cold starters, as is beef carpaccio; fried cheese and chicken wings are typical examples of warm appetisers.

Main courses are often divided into different sections, such as *gaļas ēdieni* (meat), *putnu gaļas ēdieni* (poultry) and *zivju ēdieni* (fish). *Karbonāde* – essentially a fillet with the bone still attached or pounded thin and breaded like a *schnitzel* – is by far the most popular cut of meat. Steaks are also in vogue of late, but expect to pay at least €10 for a juicy, rare, piece of beef. Fusion cooking is also quite popular in the Latvian capital, but some restaurants still believe that a main course should consist of a piece of meat with potatoes garnished with a small beetroot or carrot salad on the side or chopped tomatoes and cucumbers on a piece of lettuce. The better establishments

Fresh fish features heavily on menus

make full use of Latvia's bountiful culinary resources, so you can expect seasonal dishes made from local forest mushrooms or wild game such as boar's ribs and venison stew.

All of the usual desserts, such as ice cream, cake and fruit salads, can be found at most restaurants, but a local speciality unique to Latvia is a type of pudding called *ķīselis*, which is made from boiled oats and fruit. Fresh raspberries, strawberries and currants are often added to desserts.

NATIONAL DISHES AND SPECIALITIES

Being a nation of farmers for so many years, Latvia's national foods are, to put it mildly, rustic in nature. *Pīrāgi* are small pastry buns traditionally, although not exclusively, filled with chopped ham and onions. Others are filled with

⊙ WEEDS AND SEEDS

In the absence of any exotic spices, such as chillies, generations of Latvian mothers and grandmothers have had to make do with what the Baltic's sandy shores can offer to enliven their otherwise bland dishes of pork, cabbage and potatoes. The most ubiquitous of these is dill. The kitchens of all but the finest restaurants in Riga have giant buckets of the green weed, which is liberally applied to any dish, not excluding pizza and pasta. The second offender is caraway seeds, which are called for in nearly every Latvian recipe. They are added to salads and sauerkraut, baked into bread and meatballs and generously sprinkled on roasts of all kinds. Although restaurant staff won't understand why anyone would eat a meal without these weeds and seeds, you can nevertheless order your food *bez dillēm/ķimenēm* (without dill/caraway seeds).

minced meat, cheese and even sauerkraut and are available in most cheap cafés. A bowl of boiled grey peas fried with bacon and onions is also a favourite Latvian treat and is often topped with *kefīrs*, a dairy drink similar to yoghurt. Available at most traditional Latvian restaurants, peas are also eaten at Christmas and New Year's Eve to bring good luck in the coming year.

Piragi – bacon and onion buns

Latvians also pride themselves on a wide variety of local sausages, which, when compared to German bratwurst or knackwurst, just don't cut the mustard. However, the thin *mednieku desiņas*, or hunters' sausages, are by far the most popular type and definitely worth a try.

Many of the more unusual Latvian dishes seldom grace the pages of all but a few menus in the capital. Be on the lookout for a local delicacy often referred to as 'bulls' glands,' which is tastier than it sounds. *Grūdenis* is a thick country stew that uses a pig's head as a base.

All of the national dishes mentioned are usually complemented by a slice of delicious rye or black bread. Although difficult to find, some restaurants also offer *kaņepju sviests* or hemp butter to spread on breads. Brownish-grey in colour with a sticky consistency, it is made by grinding hemp seeds and is similar to peanut butter.

SNACKS

Any summer terrace or bar will offer a selection of local snacks that are sure to enhance your beer-drinking experience, or at least convince you to order another pint. The most popular of these is *grauzdiņi*, which consist of deep-fried black bread slathered in garlic paste. These cheap and filling snacks will definitely influence your breath, but then everyone around you will probably smell the same. A cheese platter or *sieru plate* can also be ordered at most establishments as a starter or as a snack with a drink. *Lašmaizītes* are also popular and usually consist of cured salmon on a small piece of buttered bread with dill.

The Armenian treat *basturma* is a favourite in Riga. Although legend has it that the inhabitants of the Caucasus Mountains used to make the snack from horse meat, locals make it from beef. The meat is served in thin slices and tastes a bit like American smoked or dried jerky. A dining experience at a Slavic-style restaurant is never complete without a plate of *salo*, which is flavoured bacon fat sliced into thin strips and rolled up into small cones; it tastes much better than it sounds. Dried, Russian-style fish called *voblas* are salty and rock hard, yet still amazingly popular among diners. On occasion, Latvian bars will also serve pig's ears, which are not a euphemism for something more appetising. They are considered to be a delicacy by locals.

Latvian wine

Latvia is certainly not a wine country, but it does have the distinction of having the world's northernmost vineyard, of which the natives in Sabile are very proud. The town's coat of arms even features a cluster of grapes. Imported wines are still your best bet in Riga.

DRINKS

Latvians enjoy a good drink, and beer is the undisputed favourite in Old Riga during summer. Although Aldaris, which makes several different varieties of beer, has the largest market share due to its sheer size and huge marketing budget, several smaller breweries have also gained in popularity, not least of which northern Europe's oldest brewery, Cēsu Alus, which has

Riga Black Balsam

been in operation since 1590. Užavas, Tērvetes, Piebalgas, Bauskas and Valmiermuiža are more traditional beers brewed in smaller quantities and well worth a try. Despite the country's long brewing traditions, spirits are still the most widely sold alcoholic beverages in Latvia. Latvijas Balzams produces dozens of different vodkas, brandies, whiskies and flavoured liqueurs, but its most famous product is the herbal bitter Rīgas Melnais Balzams, Riga Black Balsam (see page 86).

Kefīrs is a dairy drink similar to yoghurt and is served in the majority of cafés in the city. *Kvass*, a brown-coloured drink made from rye-bread crusts and raisins, is popular with both children and adults. *Bērzu sulas* (birch juice) is a favourite in the countryside in summer, but it looks a lot like dishwater, often gives off a curious odour and bears no similarity to birch beer. Freshly squeezed fruit juices are also widely available in Riga, as well as mineral water, both sparkling and still.

Homemade cheese

TO HELP YOU ORDER...

Could we have a table? **Vai būtu kāds brīvs galds?**
I'd like... **Man lūdzu...**
The bill, please **Rēķinu, lūdzu**

beer **alus**	pepper **pipari**
bread **maize**	potatoes **kartupeļi**
butter **sviests**	rice **rīsi**
coffee **kafija**	salad **salāti**
eggs **olas**	salt **sāls**
fish **zivs**	sandwich **sviestmaize**
fruit **augļi**	soup **zupa**
ice cream **saldējums**	sugar **cukurs**
meat **gaļa**	tea **tēja**
menu **ēdienkarte**	water **ūdens**
milk **piens**	wine **vīns**

MENU READER

ābols apple
ananass pineapple
apelsīns orange
arbūzs watermelon
avenes raspberries
biezzupa stew
burkāni carrots
cūkgaļa pork
dārzeņi vegetables
desa sausage
dilles dill
eļļa oil
etiķis vinegar
fileja fillet
forele trout
garneles shrimp
garšvielas spices
gurķis cucumber
ikri caviar
jēra gaļa lamb
kalmārs squid
kāposti cabbage
karbonāde pork chop
ķimenes caraway
ķiploki garlic
kotletes meatballs
krējums cream
kūka cake
lasis salmon
mārrutki horseradish
menca cod

mērce sauce
mīdijas mussels
ogas berries
olīvas olives
omlete omelette
pankūkas pancakes
pelmeņi dumplings
persiks peach
pīrāgi filled pastries
pupas beans
sēnes mushrooms
siers cheese
sīpols onion
šķiņķis ham
šnicele schnitzel
steiks (liellops) steak (beef)
stilbs leg
teļa gaļa veal
tītars turkey
tomāti tomatoes
trusis rabbit
tuncis tuna
vārīts boiled
vēzis crab
vīnogas grapes
vista chicken
zandarts pike-perch
zemenes strawberries
zirņi peas
zivs fish
zutis eel

PLACES TO EAT

There is a wide range of dining choices in Riga today. Although international menus seem to be the most popular choice of local restaurateurs, many establishments are dedicated to various ethnic cuisines, some with better results than others. Don't be surprised if your nachos are topped with pickles instead of jalapeño peppers.

When one considers Riga's location on the Baltic Sea in northern Europe, the lack of proper seafood offerings and the profusion of authentic Armenian cuisine is puzzling. Food from the Caucasus Mountains can be explained by the arrival of fleeing Armenian refugees after a devastating earthquake in 1988, but the absence of crabs, lobsters, oysters and other delicious creatures of the sea is still a mystery.

Dining out is still relatively inexpensive by European standards and a full Latvian meal consisting of roast pork, stewed sauerkraut and potatoes smothered in mushroom sauce seldom costs more than €6–8. A 10 percent tip is generally expected, even if the service didn't merit a few santīmi. Some restaurants automatically add a gratuity to your bill.

Opening hours for most restaurants are 11am–11pm, and a rare few are open from 8am for breakfast. Many restaurants double as bars and are open well into the night. Inexpensive two-course lunch specials, often including a soft drink, have become increasingly popular at many bars and cafés. The price ranges listed below are based on the average cost of a main course only.

€€€€€	over €25
€€€€	€14–25
€€€	€10–14
€€	€7–10
€	under €7

OLD RIGA

Bon Vivant €€€–€€€€ *Mārstaļu 8, tel: 6722 65 85,* www.bon-vivant.lv. Riga's only authentic Belgian beer bar and restaurant offers a cosy, rustic atmosphere and a fantastic menu that includes a variety of mussels, giant sausages ordered by the half metre and specialities like country beef stewed in dark beer. Several delicious brews from the Low Countries are all served in their proper glasses and the staff are friendly. Open Mon, Wed, Sun noon–11pm, Thur noon–midnight, Fri–Sat noon–1am.

Coffee-Inn €€–€€€ *Grēcinieku 11a*, http://caffeine-roasters.com. A branch of the Baltic chain also present in Lithuania, Estonia, it serves excellent Italian coffee and a selection of other drinks and snacks. Swift and efficient service. Open Mon–Thur 7am–9pm, Fri until 11pm, Sat 10am–11pm.

Folkklubs Ala Pagrabs €€ *Peldu 19, tel: 2779 69 14*, www.folkklubs.lv. This popular bar/restaurant specialises in authentic, filling Latvian fare. It's furnished in rustic style: you can either sit at a small wooden table or share a large one with strangers. As many as 27 Latvian draught beers are offered. Live concerts at least five times a week, mostly of Latvian folk music. Open Mon–Tue noon–1am, Wed noon–3am, Thur noon–4am, Fri noon–6am, Sat 2pm–5am, Sun 2pm–1am.

Gan bei €€ *Audēju 16 (Galerija Centrs), tel: 2700 05 40*, https://ganbei.lv. Sushi and many other Asian dishes are served up in this atmospheric restaurant in a trendy shopping centre in the heart of Old Riga. For those who don't fancy oriental food European meals are also available. Part of a popular oriental restaurant chain which has several other outlets across the city. Open daily 10am–10pm.

Indian Raja €€€ *Skārņu 7, tel: 6722 32 40*, www.indianraja.lv. Latvians speak an Indo-European language, but any other similarities with the people of the subcontinent end there, which explains the lack of locals here. Indian Raja is, however, full of expatriates and tourists who can't get enough of authentic curries and other traditional Indian dishes in this charming cellar restaurant that was the only establishment in Riga to make Condé Nast Traveller's list of the 'Top 100 Restaurants of Europe'. Open daily noon–11pm.

Melnie mūki €€€ *Jāņa sēta 1 (entrance from Kalēju), tel: 2997 97 29*, www.melniemuki.lv. The former personal chef to Latvia's first post-communist president creates delicious cuisine from around the globe in this elegant restaurant located in a section of a medieval convent. The menu is so extensive that it could take hours to read its entire contents, but the chef's favourite choices are highlighted and often include anecdotes about where and how he gained the recipe. Reservations recommended. Open daily noon–10pm (until last customer Fri–Sat).

Monterosso €€€€ *Vaļņu 9, tel: 6750 71 70,* www.monterosso.lv. Given the fact that this place is often filled with members of the local Italian community, it's fairly safe to say that the cuisine served here meets with their approval. Elegant wood-panelled walls, high ceilings and a general air of old-world opulence awaits, as do pizzas, pastas and main dishes with an excellent selection of Italian wines. The house special is *frutti di mare* over black pasta. Delicious pastries are also available at the cappuccino bar open from 10am. Open Mon–Thur and Sun noon–10.30pm, Fri–Sat noon–11pm.

Muusu €€€€ *Skārņu 6, tel: 2577 25 52,* www.muusu.lv. Nordic-style interior with exposed brick and wood and metal accents is a perfect setting for Kaspars Janson's haute cuisine. The menu features European contemporary classics with seasonal ingredients. Great food and ambiance. Tue and Sat 5–10.30pm, Wed–Fri 12.30–10.30pm.

Rozengrāls €€€€ *Rozena 1, tel: 2576 98 77,* www.rozengrals.lv. Although many restaurants may claim to be authentically medieval, Rozengrāls is the real thing: it is located in a 13th-century cellar once used by town officials for feasts; potatoes, tomatoes and other food that wouldn't have been available in medieval Latvia are absent from the menu and the entire staff is dressed in period costume. Local brews and curious drinks concocted from centuries-old recipes are also on offer. Open daily noon–midnight.

Soraksans €€ *Miesnieku 12, tel: 6722 90 68.* This cosy Korean restaurant decorated with paper lanterns and Oriental motifs was the first of its kind in Riga to offer authentic ethnic cuisine at prices that average Latvians could afford, and it's still incredibly popular, drawing in crowds at lunchtime. Kimchi (spicy mixed vegetables), sushi and exotic concoctions like bibimbap (rice-based mixture), served in red-hot earthenware bowls, are just some of its specialities. Open daily noon–10pm.

Tam labam būs augt €€€€ *Torna street 4, tel: 2037 05 37,* www.3pavari. lv. The name (What's good will grow) says it all. This trendy restaurant/ bar run by three popular chefs – Mārtiņš Sirmais, Ēriks Dreibants and Artūrs Trinkuns – offers some of the best modern Latvian cuisine. Most meals are prepared using slow cooking methods then served on a paper card or a granite slab by the chef himself, who is eager to unveil the culinary secrets behind his creations. The menu is short, seasonal and changes so often that even the most faddy gourmets will be satisfied. Open daily noon–11pm.

THE CENTRE

Bibliotēka №1 €€€€€ *Tērbatas 2, tel: 2022 50 00,* www.restoransbiblio teka.lv. Located in the beautiful Vērmane Park, this is one of the best restaurants in town with an exquisite interior reminiscent of the old library and excellent contemporary Latvian cuisine rich in flavours and textures. The rack of lamb is to die for, as is the duck with a lavender crust. Desserts are delicious too, try the local speciality – Beekeeper's Joy – honey, sour cream snow, pollen, honey sponge, and sea buckthorn gel. To top it all off is the excellent, award-winning, wine list (mainly Italian) and superb views over Vērmane Park. Open Mon–Sat noon–midnight, Sun 11am–4pm, 6pm–midnight.

Aragats €€€ *Miera 15, tel: 6737 34 45,* www.aragats.lv. With an absence of tasteful decorations, the interior of this family-run restaurant is decidedly Soviet era, but this is more than made up for by the attentive, friendly service and the fantastic cuisine. While the father prepares delicious kebabs over the grill or heats aromatic coffees in basins of scorching sand in the kitchen, his wife and daughter will be more than happy to make food and wine suggestions in a variety of languages and will even try to discourage you from combining certain drinks with certain dishes. Open Tue–Thur noon–10pm, Fri–Sat noon–11pm, Sun noon–7pm, Sun closed June–Aug.

Bergs €€€€ *Elizabetes 83/85 (Berga Bazārs), tel: 6777 09 57*, www.hotelbergs.lv. Even if the food is delicious, sometimes you simply can't get past the fact that you're eating in a hotel restaurant. Bergs is an exception to the rule. Modern, minimalist interior design, impeccable service and an excellent menu of fusion cuisine make it the destination for upmarket dining in Riga. If you do suddenly remember that you're in a hotel, you can take comfort in the fact that it made Condé Nast Traveller's list of the top 100 hotels in the world. Open daily 7.30am–11pm. Brunch and lunch menus are good value.

Čarlstons €€€€ *Blaumaņa 38/40, tel: 6777 05 73*, www.charlestons.lv. Of the many restaurants that local celebrity and renowned restaurateur, Canadian-Latvian Elmārs Tannis, has opened, Čarlstons is perhaps his best effort. The interior is stylish, yet warm, the innovative menu offers a wealth of international dishes for reasonable prices and the summer terrace is one of the best in the city centre. The cappuccino and pastry bar is open daily for breakfast from 8am. Open Mon–Thur noon–11pm, Fri until midnight, Sat 11am–11pm, Sun until 8pm.

Gastronome €€€–€€€€ *Krasta 68a, tel: 6701 96 19*, www.mc2.lv. This stylish grill bar offers delicious seafood from fresh oysters and scallops to steamed mussels and lobster imported from 15 countries. If you prefer to do the cooking yourself, you can also buy fresh shellfish and seafood from the Gastronome delicatessen located next door to the grill bar. Open Mon–Wed noon–9pm, Thur–Fri noon–10pm, Sat 11am–10pm, Sun 11am–5pm.

El Gaucho €€–€€€ *Vaļņu 19, tel: 6713 09 88*, http://elgaucho.lv. This is an Argentinian steakhouse so anyone who likes their steaks will be happy there. Good wines are offered to match the dishes. The interior is a blend of rustic/industrial. Open daily noon–11pm.

Italissimo €€–€€€ *Baznīcas 27/29, tel: 2656 48 67*. Tasty Italian food served in stylish surroundings. Platters of mixed grilled meat and seafood, and the tortellini are worth a try, as are their traditional mouthwatering desserts. The restaurant also offers a decent selection of Italian wines to choose from. A family-friendly place with a separate room for children who can play there with a childminder. Open daily noon–11pm.

Kabu €€€ *Tērbatas 46, tel: 2088 80 08*; www.sushi.lv. This trendy Japanese restaurant could hold its own in New York, San Francisco and maybe even Tokyo. The interior is stylishly minimalist and modern. Flaky tempura, succulent teriyakis and sashimi that melts in your mouth are all on offer as well as excellent sushi. Open Mon–Thur 11am–10pm, Fri 11am–11pm, Sat noon–11pm, Sun noon–9pm.

Riviera €€€€ *Dzirnavu 31 (entrance from Antonijas), tel: 2660 59 30*, http://rivierarestorans.lv. Located only a 15-minute walk from the Freedom Monument, Riviera is a fish lovers' paradise. The abundant choice of classic seafood dishes includes brook trout, pike perch, grilled catfish, mahi-mahi, halibut and many others. The seafood platter is perfect for groups. Meanwhile, carnivores can opt for a choice of some prime cuts cooked to perfection on the wood-fired grill. The wine list features more than 250 bottles, mainly from the Mediterranean or New World. Open daily noon–11pm.

Steiku Haoss €€€€ *Tērbatas 41/43, tel: 6727 27 07*, www.steikuhaoss.lv. If you've ever had the desire to star in a Hollywood Western, this might be the place for you. Step through the swinging saloon doors and wait for the hostess in cowboy boots and hat to seat you in front by the grill or in back by the stage where local country acts occasionally coax diners into line dancing. Huge American-style steaks are served with Idaho potatoes, but thankfully only local beer is available on draught. Open daily noon–10pm.

Vairāk saules €€ *Dzirnavu 60, tel: 6728 28 78*, www.vairaksaules.lv. Although the menus and interior of this stylish pizzeria and cocktail bar put one in mind of chain restaurants, the atmosphere is warm and the staff are incredibly friendly in a city where people seldom smile in public. In addition to pizzas, pastas, pork chops and other main dishes, a children's menu is on offer, as well as an entire menu page dedicated to Tyrolean cuisine. The restaurant's name means 'more sun', which Latvians could certainly use. Open Mon–Sat 9am–11pm, Sun 10am–10pm.

FURTHER AFIELD

Lido atpūtas centrs €–€€ *Krasta 76, tel: 6781 21 82*, www.lido.lv. Difficult to describe, the Lido Leisure Centre is a huge log cabin nearly the size of a football pitch surrounded by an amusement park with various attractions for both children and adults. Inside is what must be northern Europe's largest buffet, divided into sections, each easily recognisable by the symbol hanging above it, such as a chicken, a cow, a pig, a potato. Downstairs you can listen to live Latvian um-pa-pa bands or try one of the beers brewed on the premises. Table service is available on the top floor for anyone who wants to avoid the crowds and the sights, sounds and smells of the gigantic cauldrons bubbling over with hearty Latvian food. Open daily 11am–11pm. Cash only.

A–Z TRAVEL TIPS

A SUMMARY OF PRACTICAL INFORMATION

A

ACCOMMODATION

Quality, affordable accommodation is difficult to find in Riga. Local ho-
teliers seem to be under the mistaken impression that all Westerners
are incredibly wealthy and eager to part with their euros. Some reason-
ably priced rooms are available, but thrifty travellers should book well
in advance of their arrival date, perhaps even months ahead if planning
a visit in the summer. For those who don't mind spending over €85 per
night, Riga offers a wide range of excellent accommodation from stylish boutique hotels in refurbished medieval buildings to modern suites
with private saunas. Breakfast and 12 percent VAT are almost always
included in room rates, but hotels often charge more for rooms with
good views of Old Riga or other major tourist attractions.

Although not recommended during the summer months due to a
likely lack of availability, accommodation can also be booked upon arrival at the airport or Riga Information Centre, Rātslaukums 6, tel: 6703
79 00, www.liveriga.com. Booking a room of any price range is seldom
a chore during autumn and winter when occupancy rates plummet. In
addition to Latvian and Russian, most hotel staff speak English and
sometimes German.

A single/double room with bath/shower **Vienvietīgu/
Divvietīgu numuru ar vannu/dušas kabīni**
What's the rate per night? **Cik maksā par vienu nakti?**
Is breakfast included? **Vai brokastis ir iekļautas cenā?**

AIRPORT

Riga International Airport, known by its code as RIX, is located 13km
(8 miles) outside the city centre and is easily accessed by taxi or bus.
Substantial investment by the European Bank for Reconstruction and

Development has transformed a small concrete block of a building into a shiny glass and metal testament to modernity. In addition to the national airline airBaltic, Riga is served from London by Ryanair, Wizz Air and a few charter operators. For more information visit www.riga-airport.com.

A queue of reputable taxis is always available outside and the trip to the city centre takes roughly 20 minutes. City bus No. 22 picks up passengers on the far side of the car park when exiting the arrivals hall. Shuttle mini buses Nos 241 or 322 depart every 30 minutes for the city centre. A ticket (€2 single) can be purchased from the driver, vending machines or the airport's tourist bureau (a single ticket with e-talons rechargeable card costs €1.15). For schedules see www.rdsd.lv.

A Riga Shuttle Bus leaves every 30 minutes (10.30am–7pm) from P1 parking space in front of E gateway doors (a single ticket that can be bought from the driver costs €5).

What bus do I take to the centre? **Ar kādu autobusu man jābrauc uz centru?**
How much is the fare to...? **Cik maksā biļete līdz...?**
Will you tell me when to get off? **Lūdzu, pasakiet, kad jāizkāpj.**

B

BUDGETING FOR YOUR TRIP

Once remarkably cheap compared to Western cities, Riga has become increasingly expensive. Average prices for essentials are as follows:

Airport transfer. Taxis to the city centre cost €12–15. The trip to the centre by bus or mini bus will cost between €1.15–5.

Public transport. An e-talons rechargeable cards can be bought from ticket offices, vending machines, press kiosks and Narvesen shops. A single trip on bus/tram/trolleybus/minibus costs €1.15 (€2 when bought on-board). A five ride ticket costs €5.75, 10 rides are €10.90, and 20 rides are €20.70. Riga Pass comes in three variations (24 hour – €25, 48 hour – €30 and 72 hour – €35) and offers unlimited travel on public transport, free sightseeing tours as well as discounts in museums and restaurants. For routes, timetables and fares consult www.rigassatiksme.lv.

Car hire. A compact car with unlimited mileage costs about €30 a day. Sixt (www.sixt.lv) offers all kinds of cars, bicycles and even Vespa scooters (from €35 a day).

Hotels. Accommodation will be your greatest expense in Riga, although rooms can be ridiculously cheap outside of the capital. A bed in a common dormitory in one of the many hostels will start from €10 with a double room in a budget hotel costing at least €30. A mid-range hotel should cost an average of €80. Rates for top-end hotels begin at about €90. Breakfast and 12 percent VAT are almost always included in the price of a room. Room rates can be as much as €20 higher during the short summer season.

Meals and drinks. A main course at a typical restaurant usually costs around €5. A three-course meal for two in a mid-range restaurant will be around €40. Domestic beer can be bought at a bar for as little as €2. Cocktails can cost more than €5.

Taxis. Make sure to use only licensed taxis with yellow license plates beginning with TX or TE. Always check if the meter is turned on. The maximum day fare is €0.71 per kilometre while the initial fee is €2.15. Two reputable taxi companies are Baltic Taxi (tel: 85 00; http://baltictaxi.com) and Red Cab (tel: 83 83; www.rtp.lv). You can also book taxis from other companies by calling 371 8880.

Entertainment. Tickets to world-class opera and ballet performances, as well as classical music concerts, are relatively cheap, starting from around €5 per ticket. However, the best seats for top performances may cost up to €70.

Guided tours. A proper tour of Riga starts from €10 and day excursions to Sigulda and Rundāle Palace cost around €50.

C

CAR HIRE

There is no better way to see Latvia's beautiful natural scenery than to hire a car. If limiting your sightseeing to the capital city, hiring a car is not necessary as most of Riga's places of interest can be easily reached on foot, by bicycle or by cheap and efficient public transport. Hiring a car is simple and relatively inexpensive. You must be at least 21 years of age and must possess a valid driving licence (for at least a year), passport and major credit card. Bear in mind that many Latvians are irresponsible drivers who are not above passing on blind turns or suddenly driving in the opposite lane of oncoming traffic to avoid a pothole. Many rural roads, which account for the vast majority of Latvia's infrastructure, are in a sad state of repair. Rental agencies include:

Add Car Rental, Dzirnieku iela 6, Mārupe, tel: 2658 96 74, www.addcarrental.com.

Auto, tel: 2958 04 48, www.carsrent.lv.

Avis Airport, tel: 6720 73 53, www.avis.lv.

Sixt Airport, tel: 6720 71 21, www.sixt.lv.

Budget Rent a Car Airport, tel: 6720 73 27, www.budget.lv.

Europcar Airport, tel: 6720 78 25, www.europcar.lv.

Hertz Airport, tel: 2943 27 69, www.hertz.lv.

> I'd like to hire a car for one day/week **Es vēlos īrēt automašīnu uz dienu/nedēļu**
> Where's the nearest filling station? **Kur ir tuvākā degvielas uzpildes stacija?**
> Full tank, please **Pilnu bāku, lūdzu**

CLIMATE

The best time to visit Riga is during the summer months between mid-

May and mid-September. Winters are often wet and harsh with very little sunlight to lift the gloom. It's not uncommon for Riga to experience snow flurries as late as April.

	J	F	M	A	M	J	J	A	S	O	N	D
°C max	-2	-2	3	9	16	19	21	20	15	10	4	0
°C min	-6	-6	-3	2	7	11	13	13	9	5	1	-4
°F max	29	29	37	48	60	66	69	68	59	50	39	32
°F min	22	21	28	35	45	52	56	55	48	41	33	25

CLOTHING

Temperatures of -10°C are not uncommon during the winter months so bring a hat, gloves, warm coat and even thermals if travelling at this time. A light rain jacket or windbreaker will come in handy in both spring and summer, and warm clothing is essential in autumn. Eveningwear is expected at the opera, and some nightclubs will bar admittance to clubbers in trainers, so bring a pair of proper shoes if going out.

CRIME AND SAFETY

Riga is no more dangerous and in most respects is safer than many European capitals. Visitors should be most wary of irresponsible drivers and drunken youths in Old Riga after midnight. Organised scams and gangs of pickpockets are nearly unheard of. Avoid the unkempt hawkers of cheap or fake amber and outdated postcards that offer their wares to groups of unsuspecting tourists and foreigners; their goods are rarely the genuine article.

The most common form of petty theft is the snatching of mobile phones at beer gardens, so keep your belongings in your pockets to be on the safe side. Some unlucky expatriates have also been mugged on their way home from bars and clubs in the wee hours of the morning, so a taxi might be a good idea. It is better to avoid Maskavas (Moscow) district after dark.

I want to report a theft **Es vēlos paziņot par zādzību**
Where is the nearest police station? **Kur ir tuvākais policijas iecirknis?**
Stop thief! **Keriet zagli!**
Help! **Palīgā!**
Go away **Ejiet projām**

CUSTOMS AND ENTRY REQUIREMENTS

Passports/Visas. All citizens of the European Union as well as Canadians, Americans, Australians, New Zealanders and citizens of the SAR of Hong Kong may enter Latvia without a visa and stay up to 90 days every six months. Latvia is a member of the Schengen Zone but you should bring your passport anyway.

Vaccinations. You do not need any special vaccinations to enter Latvia, but cases of tick-borne encephalitis are not uncommon in the countryside.

Customs. Travellers (from non EU countries) are permitted to bring 200 cigarettes or 50 cigars, 4 litres of wine, 1 litre of spirits and 16 litres of beer. There are no limits on the amount of currency you may bring with you to Latvia. Amounts exceeding €10,000 should be declared when arriving from a non-EU country.

D

DRIVING

Much like the rest of the world, a valid driving licence, ID or passport, vehicle registration as well as proof of insurance are required to operate a vehicle in Latvia. There the similarities end.

Road conditions. Latvia's roads have steadily improved in recent years but catching up with Western standards might still take some time. Sadly, in terms of fatalities the Latvian roads are the worst in the entire EU (see Safety below) which is mainly due to reckless driving habits and difficult weather conditions for most of the year.

Rules and regulations. Like the rest of continental Europe, driving is on the right side of the road. In urban areas and towns the speed limit is 50kmh (30mph) and 90kmh (55–70mph) on the open road unless marked otherwise. The drink-driving limit is 0.05 percent (equivalent to a half litre of beer) or even 0.02 percent for drivers with less than 2 years' experience. Speed traps are prevalent. All drunk drivers face a mandatory 10–15 day jail sentence. Many Latvian drivers are irresponsible and think nothing of passing when their view is obscured. Driving in the oncoming traffic lane is also quite common, especially if a driver can spare their car's suspension by avoiding potholes. Make sure to have your front lights on at all times and winter tires from Dec till Mar.

Safety. Latvia has the third-highest proportion of road-accident casualties in Europe, with around 78 fatalities per 1 million inhabitants. In 2018, there were 148 road fatalities. When one considers that Latvia's population is just under 2 million and that approximately 700,000 of those people live in Riga, the statistics are staggering.

Parking. There are parking meters situated are all over the city. Rates vary according to the zone; the closer you park to Old Riga, the more

Gājēji Pedestrians
Stāvvieta Parking
Vienvirziena iela One-way street
Pa kreisi/pa labi Left/right
Bīstami Danger
Apkārtceļš Detour
Stop Stop

you must pay. Drivers must pay at the meter or by phone (SMS Riga) and place the receipt on the dashboard of their car to avoid it being clamped. Rates can be as high as €10 per hour in the old town. For details go to www.rigassatiksme.lv.

Breakdowns. Should your car experience mechanical problems, call the following toll-free number of the Latvian Automotive Society (LAMB) for 24-hour towing services, tel: 1888, www.lamb.lv.

E

ELECTRICITY

The electrical current used in Latvia is 220V AC, 50Hz. Two-pronged European plugs are necessary.

EMBASSIES

Australians and New Zealanders should contact the UK embassy.

Canada Baznīcas 20/22, tel: 6781 39 45, www.canadainternational.gc.ca.

Republic of Ireland Alberta 13, tel: 6703 93 70, www.dfa.ie/irish-embassy/latvia.

United Kingdom Alunāna 5, tel: 6777 47 00, www.gov.uk/world/organisations/british-embassy-riga.

USA Samnera Velsa 1, tel: 6710 70 00, https://lv.usembassy.gov.

Where is the British/American Embassy? **Kur ir Lielbritānijas/Amerikas vēstniecība?**

EMERGENCIES

In Riga you can dial 112 for any emergency and the operator will connect you to the appropriate authorities.

Fire: 01

Police: 02
Paramedics: 03
Tourist police 24-hour hotline: 6718 18 18
Information hotline: 1188

> Police! **Policija!**
> Fire! **Ugunsgrēks!**
> Help! **Palīgā!**
> Where can I find a doctor who speaks English? **Kur es varu atrast ārstu, kas runā angliski?**

G

GETTING THERE

By Air. The national carrier, airBaltic, www.airbaltic.com, offers affordable direct flights to Riga from London (Gatwick), Brussels, Berlin, Stockholm and several other cities in Europe. The following airlines operate flights to Riga from their local hubs: Norwegian (Oslo), Turkish Airlines (Istanbul), Lufthansa (Frankfurt), Finnair (Helsinki), Aeroflot (Moscow Sheremetevo), and LOT Polish Airlines (Warsaw). Low cost airlines now offer direct flights to Riga. Ryanair flies from London Stansted, East Midlands, Edinburgh, Leeds Bradford, Manchester and Dublin, while Wizz Air from London (Luton) and Doncaster/Sheffield. If travelling from North America, contact Scandinavian Airlines-SAS, KLM, Lufthansa, Finnair, Czech Airlines, LOT Polish Airlines and Uzbekistan Airways for the most convenient connections to Riga. If travelling from Australia or New Zealand contact KLM or Lufthansa.

By Rail. It is possible to reach Latvia by rail from Russia (Moscow, Saint Petersburg), Belarus (Minsk) and Estonia (Valga). For fares and schedules go to www.pv.lv/en/.

By Road. Eurolines www.eurolines.lt runs buses to many European cities, including London. If you're driving your own car, see page 117. Other operators include Ecolines (https://ecolines.net) and Lux Express (www.luxexpress.eu).

GUIDES AND TOURS

Riga Out There, tel: 44 208 123 2077, www.traveloutthere.com, provides regular tours of Riga, Rundāle Palace and Sigulda, in English, for groups of at least five people. They can also organise nightlife tours, shooting in a Soviet bunker and even a bobsleigh run in Sigulda. Amber Way, tel: 2947 63 36, www.sightseeing.lv, specialises in English-, German- and Russian-language tours of Riga on foot, by bus and even by boat. Tickets can be bought at the Riga Information Centre, Rātslaukums 6, and, depending on the tour, departures are from the Red Riflemen Monument or the St Roland statue opposite the information centre. Simple boat tours depart nearly every hour from the Old Riga bank of the River Daugava in the summer and usually cost €5–8. Longer boat rides may also include trips to Mežaparks and Jūrmala.

Is there an English-speaking guide? **Vai ir pieejams angliski runājošs gids?**
Can you translate this for me? **Vai jūs varat man šo pārtulkot?**

H

HEALTH AND MEDICAL CARE

If you're going to spend most of your stay in the Latvian countryside, a vaccination against tick-borne encephalitis is recommended. If, like most visitors, you don't intend on hiking in the hills of Vidzeme or camping in the lake country in Latgale, a vaccination isn't deemed necessary.

A major international health insurance policy, or at least travel insurance, is always recommended, but medication, minor emergency treatments and diagnostic tests are relatively inexpensive in Riga. Generic versions of many common over-the-counter drugs are available at most pharmacies – *aptiekas* in Latvian. Poor economic circumstances often encourage pharmacists and their staff to turn a blind eye to sales of certain medications such as antibiotics and even Viagra without a prescription. Vecpilsētas aptieka, Vaļņu 28 (entrance from Audēju), tel: 2037 74 76, is a 24-hour pharmacy in Old Riga.

The following are reputable emergency-service facilities with English-speaking doctors:

ARS Skolas 5, tel: 6720 10 07, https://arsmed.lv.

Diplomatic Service Medical Centre Elizabetes 57, tel: 6722 99 42, www.dsmc.lv. English-speaking dentists are also among the staff.

Riga Hospital Clinic Bruņinieku 5, tel: 6736 63 23.

HITCHHIKING

Carpoolworld (www.carpoolworld.com) has been operating in Latvia (and Riga) for some time now, but the classic hitchhiking is also widely accepted throughout the country. All of the usual precautions should be taken.

L

LANGUAGE

Latvian is not a Slavic language. Of all of the Indo-European tongues, modern Latvian and Lithuanian are the closest languages to Sanskrit and many words are still remarkably similar to their ancient root words. Latvians are extremely proud of their language and have safeguarded its existence and future use by acts of legislation. Although most Latvians, at least in Riga, still speak Russian, tourists should bear in mind that it is the language of their former occupiers and often not welcomed. Many Latvians over the age of 50 speak German, while the

Pronunciation of vowels and consonants
ā as in f**a**ther
ē as in **ai**lment
ī as in t**ea**time
ū as in p**oo**l
č as in spea**ch**
ļ as in fai**l**ure
ņ **as in te**n**ure**
š as in **sh**op
ž as in plea**s**ure
ģ as in en**g**ine
ķ as in **c**ute

younger generation is often eager to show off its knowledge of English. Any attempt by a foreigner to speak Latvian is often greeted with grateful surprise.

One aspect of the Latvian language is its pursuit to change foreign names and places to fit its grammatical usage. Cities like New York and

Basic Questions
How are you? **Kā jums klājas?/Kā tev iet?**
Pleased to meet you. **Prieks iepazīties.**
Do you speak English? **Vai jūs runājat angliski?**
I don't speak Latvian. **Es nerunāju latviski.**
Where is the nearest hotel/toilet? **Kur atrodas tuvākā viesnīca/tualete?**
What's your name? **Kā jūs/tevi sauc?**
My name is ... **Mani sauc ...**
What time is it? **Cik ir pulkstenis?**

Munich become Ņujorka and Minhene, while heads of state and film stars become Džordžs Bušs and Breds Pits in Latvian. International news often becomes a confusing display of linguistics, especially when events occur in Africa, Asia and the Middle East. An easy rule of thumb for foreigners is that an *s*, *is* or *š* is almost always added to the end of male names and an *a* or *e* is added the end of female names.

Another peculiarity of the language is that only place names and proper names are capitalised, so the Latvians are *latvieši*, the English are *angļi*, Sunday is *svētdiena* and June is *jūnijs*.

Pleasantries
Hello **Labdien!**
Hi **Sveiks!**
Good morning **Labrīt!**
Good evening **Labvakar!**
Goodnight **Arlabunakti!**
Goodbye **Uz redzēšanos! Čau! Atā!**
Yes **Jā**
No **Nē**
OK **Labi**
Cheers! **Priekā!**
All the best! **Visu labu!**
Thank you **Paldies**
No thank you **Nē, paldies!**

Directions
Left **pa kreisi**
Right **pa labi**
Straight **taisni**
Back **atpakaļ**

Days of the Week
Monday **pirmdiena**
Tuesday **otrdiena**
Wednesday **trešdiena**
Thursday **ceturtdiena**
Friday **piektdiena**
Saturday **sestdiena**
Sunday **svētdiena**

Numbers
1 **viens**
2 **divi**
3 **trīs**
4 **četri**
5 **pieci**
6 **seši**
7 **septiņi**
8 **astoņi**
9 **deviņi**
10 **desmit**
11 **vienpadsmit**
20 **divdesmit**
21 **divdesmit viens**
50 **piecdesmit**
100 **simts**
1000 **tūkstotis**

LGBTQ TRAVELLERS

Although some of Latvia's most prominent journalists, patrons of the arts and restaurateurs are openly gay, acceptance by the general public has still not been forthcoming. LGBTQ travellers should expect stares or perhaps giggles for public displays of affection as benign as holding hands. For information on gay nightlife visit https://topclub.lv or www.mygoldenclub.com/en/contact/, and to find out about Latvia's struggle with homophobia visit www.mozaika.lv.

M

MAPS

City maps are readily available at the Riga Tourist Information Centre (see Tourist Information, page 134). A wide selection of inexpensive maps and guides of Latvia and its other cities can be purchased at the Jāṇa Sēta Map Shop, Elizabetes 83/85, tel: 6724 08 94; www.mapshop.lv.

MEDIA

TV and radio. Local cable packages include the BBC World Service and CNN as well as a few music and sports channels in English. Not surprisingly, Riga doesn't have any English-language radio stations, but you can turn your dial to 100.5 for the BBC World Service.

Press. Most major world newspapers including the *Financial Times*, *Wall Street Journal Europe*, *New York Times International Edition*, *USA Today* and others are available at Narvesen shops and kiosks. For local news in English buy a copy of the weekly *Baltic Times* newspaper (www.baltictimes.com). *Rīga This Week* (www.rigathisweek.lv) is a free city guide with up to date listings and tourist information. *The Baltic Review* (https://baltic-review.com) offers independent news stories and in-depth analyses from around the Baltics. Of the many local city guides available throughout the Latvian capital, *Riga In Your Pocket* is the best choice, offering independent restaurant, nightlife and museum reviews as well as practical information, maps and an entertainment schedule.

MONEY

In 2014 Latvia replaced the lat (Ls) with the euro. Notes are issued in denominations of 5, 10, 20, 50, 100, 200 and 500 euros. Coins in circulation are 1, 2, 5, 10, 20 and 50 centimos and 1 and 2 euros.

Currency exchange. Currency exchanges, some open 24 hours, are widely available, especially in Old Riga. Rates vary and tend to be poorest in the touristy areas and in banks. You should always check the rates before exchanging any money, but scams and widely differing rates are rare in Riga.

Do you accept credit cards? **Vai varu maksāt ar kredītkarti?**
How much is this? **Cik tas maksā?**
I want to change some pounds/dollars into euros **Es vēlos apmainīt dažas mārciņas/dolārus eiros**
Where's the nearest bank/currency exchange office? **Kur ir tuvākā banka/valūtas maiņas punkts?**
What's the exchange rate? **Kāds ir maiņas kurss?**

Credit cards. Credit cards have become increasingly popular in Latvia and are used nearly as much as cash. Most hotels, restaurants, many shops and even taxis accept major international credit and debit cards.

ATMs. Cash machines or ATMs, known locally as *bankomāti*, are located on nearly every street corner in Old Riga and the city centre and accept all major credit and debit cards.

Travellers' cheques. Travellers' cheques are accepted at relatively few places in Riga, but you can cash them at most banks. They cannot be used as currency.

O

OPENING HOURS

With the exception of major shopping centres, which are usually open daily 10am–10pm, most shops are open 9am–5pm, shorter on weekends. Banks and government offices are generally open weekdays 9am–5pm. Most museums are open 10am–6pm (close earlier in winter) and many are closed on Mondays and even Tuesdays. Typical office hours are 9am–5pm Monday to Friday.

P

POLICE

The Latvian police force has been modernised, but stories of corruption and unprofessionalism are still not uncommon. Emergency services operators have been known to hang up on callers and a general air of apathy seems to pervade the police force. Thankfully, or not depending on your point of view, most traffic police no longer take bribes, but foreign visitors have been scooped up at various locations throughout the city for being, what the law enforcers deem, inebriated. Avoid a trip to the drunk tank at all costs. These, for the most part, are isolated incidences so you should not hesitate to contact the police if in trouble. During the summer months, police stroll the old city in great numbers making sure that tourists don't become the victims of pickpockets or muggers.

Where's the nearest police station? **Kur ir tuvākais policijas iecirknis?**
I've lost my wallet/handbag/passport **Es esmu pazaudējis savu naudas maku/rokas somu/pasi**

POST OFFICES

The main post office is located near the Freedom Monument at Brīvības bulvāris 32, tel: 6750 28 15, www.pasts.lv. At the time of press, sending a postcard to Europe and the United States cost €0.64 and €0.71, respectively.

I want to send this by airmail express **Es vēlos nosūtīt šo pa eksprespastu**
I want ...-euro/cent stamps **Es vēlos ...-eiro/centu pastmarkas**

PUBLIC HOLIDAYS

Banks and government offices are closed on the following holidays:

1 January **New Year's Day** *Jaungads*
March/April **Good Friday** *Lielā piektdiena*
March/April **Easter Sunday** *Lieldienas*
March/April **Easter Monday** *Otrās Lieldienas*
1 May **Labour Day** *Darba svētki*
4 May **Proclamation of Independence (1990)** *Neatkarības atjaunošanas diena*
23–24 June **Midsummer** *Līgo & Jāņi*
18 November **Independence Day (1918)** *Neatkarības atjaunošanas diena*
24–26 December **Christmas** *Ziemassvētki*
31 December **New Year's Eve** *Vecgada vakars*

PUBLIC TRANSPORT

All public transport in Riga, including trams, buses, and trolley-buses, costs a flat charge of €1.15 (€2 if bought from the driver) for the duration of your trip, regardless of how far you travel. If you get off a tram and hop on the next available one you will have to pay for another ticket. Large pieces of luggage, as well as bicycles, may be subject to an additional fee. Tickets can be purchased from the conductors on board buses. However, you are expected to buy tram and trolleybus tickets at kiosks and newsstands before travelling. There are many different options: tickets allowing for one to five rides or one to five days of unlimited travel. All tickets must then be time stamped at one of the electronic readers as soon as you get on board. The green light will flash and the display will show how many more rides are left on the card. For more information in English visit the Tram and Trolleybus Authority's excellent website, www.rigassatiksme.lv.

Minibuses called *mikroautobusi*, or *mikriņi* for short, can also be a convenient way of travelling, as they will stop at any point along a given route. But they are slightly more expensive and make frequent stops to pick up more passengers when the small van is already packed like a tin of sardines.

Trams. Electric trams have been in use in Riga since 1901. Today, there are 8 different tramlines, numbered 1, 2, 3, 5, 7, 9, 10 and 11, which together cover 182km (113 miles) of Riga. More than 270 trams service a total of over 33 million passengers each year. Trams operate from 5am to midnight, and night trams are in service approximately every hour on weekend nights.

Trolleybuses. There are 17 different trolleybuses one can take to destinations near and far. The same rules for trams apply to trolleybuses.

How much is the fare to...? **Cik maksā biļete līdz...?**
I want a ticket to ... single (one-way)/return (round-trip) **Es vēlos biļeti vienā virzienā/turp un atpakaļ**
How long does the journey take? **Cik ilgi ir jābrauc?**
Will you tell me when to get off? **Lūdzu, pasakiet, kad jaizkāpj.**

Taxis. Respectable firms should charge no more than €2.15 for pick up, €0.71 (daytime) per kilometre. Always insist on the meter being turned on or agree on a price beforehand. Lady Taxi (www.ladytaxi.lv), tel: 88 55, Smile Taxi (www.smiletaxi.lv), tel: 2233 03 30, and Rīgas Taksometru Parks (Red Cabs; www.rtp.lv), tel: 83 83, are highly regarded and will pick up passengers anywhere in Riga. Women worried about dodgy cab drivers should definitely choose Lady Taxi as most of its cabs are driven by female drivers.

You can also wave down taxis on any street, but it might be a good idea to negotiate a price before sitting down in the car. All official taxis must display a yellow number plate. The taxis at the railway and bus stations are notoriously dishonest, but the cabs at the airport are reputable.

How much is it to…? **Cik maksā līdz…?**
Take me to this address **Lūdzu, brauciet uz šo adresi**
Please stop here. **Lūdzu, apstājieties v maksu v maksu šeit.**

R

RELIGION

Christianity replaced the pagan animistic religion of Latvia in the 13th and 14th centuries. Since the Reformation, Lutheranism has been the country's dominant religion, although Orthodox Christianity and Catholicism are also widely practised, especially in eastern Latvia. Riga is also home to one of the oldest surviving groups of Old Believers in the world. Judaism in Latvia was all but destroyed by the Nazis during World War II. The Soviets persecuted clerics and followers of any religion and many of the nation's historic places of worship were converted into concert halls and museums. Since independence, churches have been restored and returned to their congregations.

T

TELEPHONES

Latvia's telecommunications system is state of the art. Increased demand for mobile phone numbers has prompted the government to change numbers from seven digits to eight. Fixed landlines have also moved to an eight-digit system and toll-free 800 numbers have been given an extra zero.

To call Latvia from abroad, dial your country's international dialling code (00 within Europe) and Latvia's country code (371), followed by the number, minus the first (0) of the area code. To call abroad from Latvia dial 00, the country code, and then the number, minus the first (0) of the area code.

Public phones. Public phones are still available in some places across the city, but a phone card is required to operate them. Cards can be bought at most kiosks and shops which display the *telekarte* sign. You can also use a credit card to make a call from a phone booth – just follow the instructions in English inside.

Mobile phones. Latvians don't seem able to live without their mobiles, and bars and restaurants are filled with lonely patrons texting their friends. For citizens of 31 European Economic Area countries, roaming charges for temporary roaming were abolished in mid-2017, yet under a fair-use policy some restrictions on the free use of mobile phones are still in place. It's always best to ask your local GSM provider before travelling.

TICKETS

Tickets for world-class performances of the opera and ballet, as well as classical concerts, are usually only available at the venue's box-office, but are almost always relatively affordable. Tickets for international pop music concerts and other large events on the other hand are often expensive by local standards. Tickets for these events can usually be purchased at the information desk at the railway station and at the customer service desk at Stockmann, 13 janvāra 8, www.bilesuserviss.lv.

TIME ZONES

Latvia is in the Eastern European Time zone, which is GMT +2 hours. An hour is added between the end of March and October for daylight savings, so during the summer local time is GMT +3 hours, known as Eastern European Summer Time or EEST for short.

New York	London	**Riga**	Jo'burg	Sydney	Auckland
6am	11am	**1pm**	1pm	10pm	midnight

TIPPING

Latvians are warming up to the idea of tipping, but many only round up to the nearest euro. Foreigners, however, are expected to leave 10 percent for good service and some menus warn customers that a gratuity will be automatically added to the bill. See if the bill includes service before leaving a tip.

TOILETS

Many public toilets throughout the city are in a sad state. If you're looking for a little piece of the Soviet past, then pay the €0.30 charge and descend into the depths of filthy tiled cellars that reek of urine, ammonia and other things that will remain unmentioned. The only exceptions are the toilets at the train station and on Līvu Square, but restaurants, cafés and hotel lobbies are still your best option. Men's and women's toilets are usually designated with a triangle pointing down or up, respectively.

Where are the toilets? **Kur ir tualetes?**

TOURIST INFORMATION

Although limited information can be gleaned from a variety of unofficial sources at the airport and at bus and train stations, the best place to find tourist information is the Riga Information Centre, Rātslaukums 6, tel: 6703 79 00, www.liveriga.com. For a full list of Latvian information centres visit www.latvia.travel. For maps and information about restaurants, nightlife, museums and local events pick up a copy of the excellent *Riga In Your Pocket* city guide, which is published once every two months.

W

WEBSITES

The official Riga tourist site (www.liveriga.com) contains essential information on the city as well as up-to-date news on concerts, performances, events, etc. For general information about Latvia, its traditions, history and language, visit the Latvian Institute's website, www.li.lv or www.latvia.travel/en. For local news from the three Baltic capitals in English visit www.baltictimes.com. A good source of information for what's on in Riga is also www.inyourpocket.com.

Y

YOUTH HOSTELS

The advent of low-cost airlines has heralded an unprecedented proliferation of quality youth hostels to accommodate the financially challenged. Travellers can take their pick of affordable beds in dorm rooms which seldom cost more than €10–12 per person.

Riga Old Town Hostel Vaļņu 43, tel: 6722 34 06, www.rigaoldtownhostel.lv.
The Naughty Squirrel Kalēju 50, tel: 6722 00 73, http://thenaughtysquirrel.com.
Central Hostel E. Birznieka-Upīša 20, tel: 2232 26 63, www.centralhostel.lv.

RECOMMENDED HOTELS

New four- or five-star hotels seem to pop up every year in Riga, but quality, affordable accommodation in the most desirable locations of Old Riga and the centre is decidedly more difficult to find. Thankfully, the growing demand for these establishments has inspired a few local entrepreneurs to open bed and breakfasts within walking distance of major sights, and a number of genuine backpacker-style hostels have opened their doors in the medieval heart of Riga. Although booking a room in autumn or winter is seldom a problem, an acute lack of mid-range hotels makes careful planning for the summer absolutely essential. Some of the most upmarket hotels offer disabled-friendly rooms, but these are few and far between. Breakfast and 12 percent VAT are almost always included in room rates, and the prices listed below are for a standard double. All of the hotels listed accept credit cards.

If calling Riga from abroad, add your country's international dialling prefix followed by Latvia's international country code 371 and then the number listed in this guide.

€€€€€	over €180
€€€€	€120–180
€€€	€80–120
€€	€60–80
€	under €60

OLD RIGA

St. Peter's Boutique Hotel €€€€ *Peldu 23, tel: 6722 30 27*, http://stpeter shotel.lv. One of Riga's best boutique hotels located just a few steps from one of Riga's most popular sights – St. Peter's Church. This beautiful 15th century building features stunning architectural details, such as wooden beams and old brick walls. Each room is decorated with style and elegance. Breakfast is served in the cellar with vaulted ceilings and a quiet drink can be had under medieval oak beams by a roaring fire in the lobby. Like most places in the old city, the street can become a bit noisy with inebriated youths on weekend nights. 22 rooms.

Avalon Hotel €€€€ *13. janvāra iela 19, tel: 6716 99 99,* www.hotelavalon. eu. This excellent hotel on the edge of Old Riga provides a breathtaking, eight-storey atrium and luxurious rooms that include tasteful interior design, satellite TV, wireless internet access, mini-bar, private bathrooms and double-glazed windows that really do prevent the sounds of the nearby train station from disturbing your sleep. An upmarket restaurant is also available, as well as a banquet room on the sixth floor with views of the Central Market. 111 rooms.

Rixwell Centra €€€–€€€€ *Audēju 1, tel: 6722 64 41,* www.rixwell.com. Although one of the city's most popular nightclubs once occupied three floors of this charming building, not a scrap of its recent past remains. The hotel offers incredibly spacious rooms, refreshingly decorated in minimalist style, often with excellent views of Old Riga's famous red-tiled roofs. The staff is friendly and professional. 27 rooms.

Forums €€ *Vaļņu 45, tel: 6781 46 80,* http://stpetershotel.lv. Close to the bus and railway stations as well as Old Riga's best bars and restaurants, Forums is a good choice for both budget travellers and those looking for a little more luxury in their lives. Standard amenities include satellite TV, phone, writing desk and en suite bathrooms with bathtubs, but if you're willing to splurge you can also choose the superior double room with its own sauna and sprawling balcony. 32 rooms.

Grand Palace Hotel €€€€€ *Pils 12, tel: 6704 40 00,* www.grandpalace riga.com. One of the city's most salubrious hotels, the Grand Palace certainly lives up to its noble name – just ask Sting, Catherine Deneuve and many other celebrities where they rest their heads when visiting Riga. The rooms offer everything that one could possibly want from such an establishment, and one of the Latvian capital's most celebrated restaurants is also at your disposal. 56 rooms.

Hotel Gutenbergs €€€ *Doma laukums 1, tel: 6781 40 90,* www.hotel gutenbergs.lv. Tucked away in a charming courtyard directly opposite the entrance to the largest cathedral in the Baltic states, you simply can't ask for a more central location than Hotel Gutenbergs. This elegant establishment offers spacious rooms with all of the usual modern conveniences and tasteful décor that often reflects the building's ancient past. Disabled-friendly and allergy-free rooms are also available as well as a top-notch restaurant and a rooftop terrace with stunning views in the summer. 38 rooms.

Hotel Roma €€€–€€€€€ *Kaļķu 28, tel: 6749 1500,* http://hotelroma.lv. You can't get much more central than Roma, which offers upmarket accommodation with a mix of modern Europe and old-world charm. All of its tastefully decorated rooms, whether they be singles, business class or suites, are spacious and offer all of the standard amenities one would expect from a five-star hotel. The restaurant on the top floor provides one of Riga's best dining experiences, with fantastic views of the Freedom Monument, opera house and the Riga Canal. Disabled-friendly rooms available. 88 rooms.

Rija Domus Hotel €€–€€€ *Tirgoņu 9, tel: 6735 82 54,* www.rijahotels. com. Only a stone's throw from Dome Square and some of the city's best pubs and restaurants, this charming hotel offers surprisingly affordable accommodation in the heart of Old Riga. Each room is slightly different in size owing to the age of the historic building and amenities include satellite TV, phone, writing desk, en suite bathrooms and tasteful minimalist décor. Top-floor attic rooms also provide much-needed air conditioning in the summer. 41 rooms.

Rixwell Konventa Sēta €€€ *Kalēju 9/11, tel: 6708 75 01,* www.rixwell. com. In medieval times the 'Convent Yard' was a convent and home for poor women and widows who could no longer support themselves. Today this complex of quaint courtyards and historic buildings makes up the core of a unique hotel that offers comfortable rooms with modern amenities and traditional touches like original oak beams. Apartments are available for long-term stays.

Hotel Neiburgs €€€€–€€€€€ *Jauniela 25/27, tel: 6711 55 22,* www. neiburgs.com. Located In the most beautiful art nouveau building, the

Neiburgs has 55 simple and stylish apartments with numerous original features dating back to the beginning of 20th century, including parquet flooring. The views of the Old Town are an additional asset. A good restaurant, run by a young chef offers local cuisine and an excellent wine list.

SemaraH Metropole €€€ *Aspazijas bulvāris 36/38, tel: 6611 9339*, www.semarahhotels.com. This impressive building on the edge of the old city houses the oldest continuously running hotel in Riga. Rooms are stylish and comfortable with all of the standard amenities. An upmarket restaurant De Commerce Gastro Pub 1871, business centre as well as a conference room are all onsite.

Radi un Draugi €€€ *Mārstaļu 1/3, tel: 6782 02 00*, www.hotelradiundraugi.lv. This surprisingly affordable hotel, owned by a Latvian expatriate organisation in the UK, was so popular with visitors that it decided to buy the neighbouring building to expand its capacity. Relatives and Friends (as the name translates) is an excellent choice offering the best value for money. It also has a good restaurant. Book well in advance. 71 rooms.

Vecrīga €€€ *Gleznotāju 12/14, tel: 6721 60 37*. Located on one of the Old Town's narrowest and most charming streets, this small hotel offers 16 comfortable, tastefully-decorated rooms which are nearly identical to one another. If you're looking for a quiet place to rest your head in the medieval heart of Riga, away from the busy beer gardens and sprawling souvenir stands, then this is the place for you. Famous guests have included the Dalai Lama and John Malkovich.

THE CENTRE

AC Hotel Riga €€€€ *Dzirnavu 33, tel: 6733 17 17*, www.marriott.com. A derelict multi-storeyed Soviet office building has been transformed into one of Riga's best hotels. Fully redesigned in 2019, the hotel now boasts 239 stylishly furnished modern rooms and suites. The 11th floor conference room has incredible views and the AC Riga Lounge offers Spanish tapas and snacks.

Teater City Hotel €€€ *Bruņinieku 6, tel: 6731 51 40,* www.cityhotel.lv. The most impressive feature of this relatively new hotel, named after its location on Knights' Street, is its amazing reception area, which is the inner courtyard of the building complex covered in glass. All of the rooms are tastefully decorated with modern amenities. A luxurious sauna and a top-floor restaurant are also available. 68 rooms.

Rija VEF €€ *Brīvības 199c, tel: 6716 60 00,* www.rijahotels.com. This modern hotel, which is slightly reminiscent of a very large submarine, is only a short tram ride from the city centre and Old Riga. Each of its affordably priced rooms includes cable TV, mini-bar, internet access and even private bathrooms with phones. 135 rooms.

Hotel Bergs €€€€€ *Elizabetes 83/85 (Berga Bazārs), tel: 6777 09 00,* www.hotelbergs.lv. Named one of the world's best hotels by Condé Nast Traveller, this designer hotel has spared no expense to bring its guests the very best in quality and service. Located in the city's trendiest outdoor shopping plaza, Hotel Bergs offers dozens of rooms which would be best described as apartment suites. Not surprisingly, its restaurant is also one of Riga's best. 37 rooms.

Laine €€ *Skolas 11, tel: 6728 9823,* www.laine.lv. Laine is an excellent choice for budget travellers, although its colour schemes, such as canary yellow and mauve, and the elaborate tile work in its bathrooms, are a bit bizarre. But the staff couldn't be friendlier or more helpful and guests have the choice of more luxurious surroundings on the upper floors or more spartan rooms on the third floor, with shared toilets and showers. 35 rooms.

Opera Hotel & Spa €€€€ *Raiņa bulvāris 33, tel: 6706 34 00,* www.opera hotel.lv. Located in an historic Art Deco building close to the Latvian National Opera and Old Riga, this 4-star hotel is in a great location and offers the luxury and relaxation of a spa, with baths and a pool and an extensive spa treatment menu.

Radisson Blu Elizabete Hotel €€€€ *Elizabetes 73, tel: 6778 55 55,* www. radissonblu.com. This modern glass and steel hotel is located opposite one of Riga's most popular green areas – Vermanes Park – a short walk from the Old Town. All of its rooms were decorated by a trendy London design firm and include either views of the park or the airy courtyard below. The usual four-star amenities are available including free wireless internet access as well as coffee and tea provisions. An upmarket grill bar and restaurant is also at your disposal. 228 rooms.

Radisson Blu Hotel Latvija €€€–€€€€ *Elizabetes 55, tel: 6777 22 22,* www.radissonblu.com. This very popular hotel has rooms offering every amenity you would expect from a four-star establishment, as well as excellent views. A trip to the 27th floor Skyline Bar is an absolute must for any visitor to the city, guest or not. A new wing with a shopping plaza and conference centre has also been added. 571 rooms.

MOSCOW DISTRICT

Dodo Hotel € *Jersikas 1, tel: 6724 02 20,* www.dodohotel.com. Opened in 2008 by two Frenchmen, this modern, no-frills hotel is perhaps Riga's first successful attempt at proper budget accommodation. Each of its many rooms provides flat-screen TVs, writing desks, a bed, wireless internet access, private bathrooms and not much else. For an additional cost, guests can also take advantage of the hotel's continental breakfast, which includes crêpes. Although finding Dodo on a map may seem like a chore, it's actually only a few tram stops from Old Riga. 109 rooms.

Hanza Hotel €€€ *Elijas 7, tel: 6779 60 40,* www.hanzahotel.lv. This hotel in a beautifully restored 19th-century building provides the best accommodation in this part of town. Located on a quiet square in the shadow of a lovely wooden church, the Hanza offers modern rooms, decorated in warm earth tones, with satellite TV, wireless internet and bathrooms with heated tile floors. Its cosy cellar pub is also a great place for a drink or an inexpensive lunch or dinner. 80 rooms.

PARDAUGAVA

Bellevue Park Hotel €€€ *Slokas 1, tel: 6706 90 00,* www.hotelbellevue. lv. This enormous hotel is situated near one of the largest city's parks and offers all the comfort amenities, including cable TV, climate control, mini-bar and a balcony with a view. It also has a spa, fitness and conference centres. Good packages for golf and horse riding lovers. 222 rooms.

Islande Hotel €€€ *Ķīpsalas 2, tel: 6760 80 00*, www.islandehotel.lv. When one looks at the Islande Hotel with its shiny glass, wood and steel facade, it's hard to believe that it was once a Soviet-style student dormitory. Its lobby looks like a modern art gallery and its well-appointed rooms are classic examples of Scandinavian minimalism. A fitness centre is also available, not to mention a bowling alley in the basement. It has a lobby bar, two restaurants and a summer terrace with a great panoramic of Old Riga. 205 rooms.

Radisson Blu Daugava €€€€ *Kuģu 24, tel: 6706 11 11,* www.radissonblu. com. This was the first international business-class hotel to open its doors in Riga, though many would argue on the wrong side of the river. Although a cab ride or a walk across the Akmens Bridge is required to reach the old city, the Radisson's location does afford it an unadulterated view of the bright yellow castle of the ancient Livonian Order and the soaring spires of numerous churches – a definite plus. Naturally, rooms facing Old Riga are more expensive than the ones facing the dilapidated industrial section of town behind the hotel. 354 rooms.

INDEX

INSIGHT ⊙ GUIDES POCKET GUIDE

RIGA

First Edition 2019

Editor: Tatiana Wilde
Author: Martins Zaprauskis
Head of DTP and Pre-Press: Rebeka Davies
Layout: Aga Bylica
Managing Editor: Carine Tracanelli
Picture Editor: Tom Smyth and Aude
Vauconsant
Cartography Update: Carte
Update Production: Apa Digital
Photography Credits: Alamy 58, 99; Getty
Images 1, 4TL, 6R, 17, 22, 60, 84; iStock 4MC,
4ML, 5T, 5TC, 7TL, 29, 34/35, 37, 47, 48, 55, 64,
75, 76, 87; Melnie Mūki 6TL; Micah Sarut/Apa
Publications 5M, 6TR, 7TR, 11, 24, 62, 70, 73,
79, 83, 97, 102; Photoshot 91; Public domain
14, 19, 21; Reinis Hofmanis/Investment
and Development Agency of Latvia 5MC;
Shutterstock 4TC, 5MC, 5M, 26, 28, 31, 33,
36, 41, 42, 44, 50, 51, 52, 53, 56, 66, 68, 77, 80,
89, 92, 95, 101; Girts Raģelis/Investment and
Development Agency of Latvia 12, 39
Front Cover: iStock
Back Cover: iStock

Distribution

UK, Ireland and Europe: Apa Publications
(UK) Ltd; sales@insightguides.com
United States and Canada: Ingram
Publisher Services; ips@ingramcontent.com
Australia and New Zealand: Woodslane;
info@woodslane.com.au
Southeast Asia: Apa Publications (SN) Pte;
singaporeoffice@insightguides.com

Worldwide: Apa Publications (UK) Ltd;
sales@insightguides.com

**Special Sales, Content Licensing
and CoPublishing**
Insight Guides can be purchased in bulk
quantities at discounted prices. We can
create special editions, personalised jackets
and corporate imprints tailored to your
needs. sales@insightguides.com;
www.insightguides.biz

Contact us
Every effort has been made to provide
accurate information in this publication,
but changes are inevitable. The publisher
cannot be responsible for any resulting loss,
inconvenience or injury. We would appreciate
it if readers would call our attention to any
errors or outdated information. We also
welcome your suggestions; please contact
us at: hello@insightguides.com
www.insightguides.com

Plan & book
your tailor-made trip
created by local
travel experts at
insightguides.com/holidays

STEP 1

Pick your dream destination
and submit an enquiry.

STEP 2

Fill in a form, sharing your travel
preferences with a local expert.

STEP 3

Receive a trip proposal, which you
can amend until you are satisfied.

STEP 4

Book securely online. Pack your
bags and enjoy your holiday!

DON'T MISS OUT
BOOK NOW AT
INSIGHTGUIDES.COM/HOLIDAYS